CAMP UK 10/2012

THE ULTIMATE POST-2012 UNIVERSITY SURVIVAL GUIDE (UK EDITION)

CAMP UK 10/2012

THE ULTIMATE POST-2012 UNIVERSITY SURVIVAL GUIDE (UK EDITION)

VLAD MACKEVIC

EDITED BY BONITA J. ELLIS

PUBLISHED IN ASSOCIATION WITH

WWW.THELECTUREROOM.CO.UK

AND WWW.FIRSTYEARCOUNTS.COM

CONTENTS

INTRODUCTION

ATTEN-TION!

Say goodbye to your old life. Forget everything that you've learnt before because life starts anew here. Welcome to Camp UK 10/2012. If you thought it was going to be easy, think again.

After so many years of hard work, sleepless nights spent revising for your A-Levels, preparation and worrying, you've finally made it to university. You are probably looking forward to your new life, possibly away from home. You could be feeling a little nervous. Whatever your expectations are, prepare to be surprised.

I've written this book in order to surprise you, and maybe even shock you, to make you think and to help you. The information it contains will blow your mind! I have to tell you right from the start that you are reading it at your own risk. But it's a risk that is totally worth taking.

This book tells you the truth about university and about the real world out there. It tells you about the challenges that modern students face and about ways to overcome them.

Let's start with the bad stuff. In the past (it can already be called 'distant'), it was enough to walk into a company waving a piece of paper that proved you had listened to lectures for three years and obtained your degree, and you would be hired almost immediately. Having a degree was the key to a skilled job.

Nowadays, things have changed. Modern students and graduates are facing four main challenges during and after their university lives:

1. Too many graduates and too few jobs

Let's face it: everyone has a degree nowadays. Universities offer courses in everything – from accounting to Zulu studies – and hundreds of thousands of young people with a Bachelor's degree enter the job market every year.

Moreover, competition among graduates with good degrees is tough: in 2011, one in seven graduates was awarded a first class and over half of those finishing university ended up with a 2:1.

In the meantime, the number of vacancies is not keeping up with the number of graduates. Every year, a number of graduates remain unemployed, have to do unpaid work for the sake of work experience (which not everyone can afford) or stay in jobs where they cannot realise their full potential. The competition for good jobs is also threateningly high: a single vacancy can easily receive 200 applications, and in areas like law or financial services the number is double or even triple.

So, all new students who enter university in 2012, as well as those who started earlier, face the same problem: how do you stand out? How can you be better than your neighbour who is also going to get a 2:1? How do you attract an employer who filters the applications based only on academic achievement?

2. Too many unfilled vacancies

Isn't it a paradox? So many graduates, so few jobs – and still, employers struggle to fill the vacancies. How is it even possible? Why is this happening?

The answer is very simple: graduates fail to match the employers' requirements. According to recent surveys carried out by the Association of Graduate Recruiters, employers' demands become stricter as competition toughens. At the same time, students do perform well academically but fail on 'soft skills' such as efficient written and spoken communication, teamwork, interpersonal skills, active on-the-job learning, work ethic and others.

The biggest problem of modern students and graduates is not unemployment, but unemployability caused by the lack of necessary skills.

There are many ways to acquire 'soft skills', and I will talk about them in detail here. One of the ways is by having *any* job, paid or unpaid. By merely being in the world of work, you can pick up basic skills and contacts (networking also seems to be one of the best ways to learn what's available). Moreover, you can also develop these skills by performing well academically and getting involved in university life beside your studies.

But how do you get that first job? And even if you do, will this bartender/waitress/sales associate experience really matter when it comes to a serious job interview? How do you *make it matter*? And how do you acquire those 'soft skills' for the time when you will need them?

This leads to the third challenge:

3. Everyone demands work experience

Yes, almost all employers say that they will only consider those applicants for graduate and even placement positions who already have some work experience – ideally, it should also be relevant.

It's easy to explain why this is the case. First of all, recruiters want serious, committed individuals who are not afraid of hard work, are willing to learn new skills and already know what it means to have a job and to show up every day, no matter if you feel like getting up or not.

If the latter is fine with you, then the following questions arise:

1. How do you get work experience while you're still an undergraduate?

2. How do you get *serious* work experience that extends beyond the range of so-called 'usual student jobs'?

3. How can you draw benefit from every little bit of work experience you have got?

4. University is becoming more and more expensive

Education costs are soaring. The generation of the year 2012 will have to pay £9,000 per year in university tuition fees and, as a result, will accumulate substantial debt by the time they graduate.

The problems are obvious: how can you make the most out of your time at university? How do you make every hour of every day count towards your degree, towards your employability, and towards your future? How to make sure that you get your money's worth from your degree course?

I will tell you the truth: university offers a lot for your tuition fees. You just need to know where to find what you need and how to make best use of it.

Naturally, the current economic and educational climate is not the easiest one, both for those entering university this year and for those who are already studying. The problems I have listed above are likely to stay the same in the years to come.

The good news is that you are holding the answers in your hands. I have written this book because I would like to share my own experience – what I have observed in myself and my classmates whilst at university – with you. I want to tell you what I wish I had known when I was an undergraduate. A lot of advice I am giving in this book came to me one way or another long after my graduation.

However, your generation cannot afford to wait till graduation. You have to take things seriously right from the start – from the first days of the first year.

The advice found here will help you gain an advantage and compete even with older graduates. It will help you become a professional from the first day of the first year. This book answers the main questions all current undergraduate students are asking:

- How do I stand out in the crowd of graduates where everyone has a good degree and some work experience?
- How do I obtain valuable transferable skills that all employers demand?
- How do I gain some serious work experience that extends beyond the range of usual student jobs?
- How do I get my money's worth out of university? What am I really paying for?
- How do I use every opportunity to develop personally, academically and professionally so that my time is spent in the most efficient manner?

I am ready to give you the answers. I have written this book with a view to helping you become more employable and prepared for real life than you could have ever imagined. However, before we start, I would like to point out a couple of things. First of all, this book is entirely subjective. It is largely based on my personal experience. I cannot guarantee that having read it you will immediately get a great job. What I can say, however, is that those who do nothing, get nowhere.

So, let's start with the basics – what you need to do to get where you want to be.

CHAPTER 1

THE BIGGEST LIE IN YOUR (UNIVERSITY) LIFE

This is one of those moments you might remember for the rest of your life. It is celebration time and all family members are calling to congratulate you. After years of hard work, revision, probably one or two sleepless nights, you've *finally made it to university*.

Congratulations once again! You arrive on campus, hardly able to believe your luck – three years full of adventures that will change your life lie ahead of you. You are excited. You are proud. You are slightly worried. You brace yourself for a new life.

And then it happens.

As soon as the rumbling of the engine of your parents' car abates in the distance, as soon as you step into the crowd, ready to plunge into the new life headfirst – you are told something that is probably the biggest lie you will ever hear during your university life.

This lie sounds too good for you to start doubting it – and this where its danger lies. It is capable of turning an optimistic, determined, enthusiastic fresher into a lazy couch potato and opportunity waster.

This lie is: *the first year of university does not count.*

One of the reasons why I have written this book is because I want to counter this lie and protect all students from the danger it poses.

It is a dangerous lie because... it's partially true. I agree that the first year of university sometimes feels like 'a gap year you never intended to take' – especially after all the A-level related pressure. However, everyone who does a gap year decides to spend it in a different way: some just choose to indulge in travelling and making their gap year one big party; others go to the Third World and help building a school or a hospital in a local village. It is up to you how you spend your time.

Yes, the grades of your first year do not count towards your final grade at the end of your final year (although currently it is being planned to revolutionise the system by introducing new 'report cards' and redesigning degree classification systems altogether). However, too many Freshers are tricked into believing that they can just keep having fun, doing the bare minimum of schoolwork needed to pass the first year, and watching television and playing sports in all the time that remains.

I have to disappoint you – life's not that easy any more. This lifestyle might have been acceptable 10 years ago, but now the situation is too desperate to continue living like that.

The first year *does count* and its significance is paramount. The most obvious reason why it counts is because it's *your time*. Imagine someone told you that one year of your life is worthless; that the effort you make during that time counts for nothing. How would this make you feel? How would you react? I can bet you'd challenge this person because your time is worth *everything* for you. You wouldn't be at university unless you thought it was worth your time. You are also reading this book because you think it's worth investing your time in it.

Moreover, imagine this situation:

You are applying for a summer internship at the end of your first year or start looking for a work placement at the start of your second year.

Most probably, your employer will want to see your academic credentials, especially if you have little or no relevant work experience. What are you going to tell your future boss? 'Hey, look here, I got 54% average in the first year, but in the second year I promise to have no less than 68%'?

No one's going to fall for that.

Therefore, unless you are not planning to do an internship or gain any work experience at all (which is the worst thing you can do), the grades of the first year *do* count.

Moreover, even though your first year grades do not count towards your academic progress (which is also likely to change in the future, looking at the current education reforms), it is still worth making more effort in the first year because many second year modules are based on what you learn in your first year. In other words, the better you perform in the beginning, the less effort you will have to make later. If you need more information on how to obtain higher grades without snapping from overwork in the process, you can find great tips in my book *From Confusion to Conclusion: How to Write a First-Class Essay.* Free samples of the book as well as related articles can be downloaded from my website:

www.FirstYearCounts.com

as well as from the website I write for:

www.TheLectureRoom.co.uk

Yet, there is no need to study to the point of exhaustion. The best way is to find a healthy balance between your studies and extra-curricular activities (I will talk a lot about those in this book!). Since the grades of the first year are not nearly as important for your academic progress as those of the second or the final year, I strongly advise you to spend as much time as you can allow developing non-academic skills by 'doing a lot of stuff' – engaging in extra-curricular activities with clubs and societies and gaining serious work experience.

In summary, your first year does count. It counts towards your studies, your skills, your work experience and, above all, your future. I have written this book to show you how to *make it count* and gain maximum advantage, taking all the benefits you can from your university life, starting from the first day of the first year. Read on and find out how to do it!

CHAPTER 2

WHOM WAS THIS BOOK WRITTEN FOR?

This book was written for all students who want to make it big at university – for everyone who wishes to develop their skills, become more employable and have a lot of fun in the process.

Yet, above all, I would like to highlight a very special part of my readership: students who, for one reason or another, chose to study what some would call 'a soft subject'. These include:

- Social Sciences (Sociology, Social Work, Politics, International Relations, etc.)
- Creative Studies (Film Studies, Media Studies, Creative Writing, Journalism, Art Design, Fine Arts, etc.)
- The Humanities (English Language and Literature, History, Philosophy, Classics, Theology and other subjects whose aim is to teach you to read between the lines)
- Foreign Languages (although those subjects can hardly be called 'soft'. As we all know, languages are difficult subjects!)
- Business Studies (especially general business administration and marketing)

I have chosen to include the last category because nowadays even a good business degree is no longer a guarantee of a good graduate position in the field. Be it investment banking or simple administrative office work, both are extremely hard to get into.

However, even if you have chosen to study a focused, rigorous subject like law, finance, engineering, mathematics, medicine, biology or natural sciences like physics or chemistry, please do not close the book yet. Just flick through the pages – it will take you only a few minutes, and even scientists may find some advice on employability which might be of particular interest to them.

So, why am I specifically targeting those groups?

Because, in my view, they are the most vulnerable when it comes to the harsh competition in the job market. Those studying medicine-related subjects, law or finance have always been fewer and, hence, faced less competition. Moreover, for most of those people, the career path has been pretty straightforward: study hard, get a prestigious internship in a high-profile organisation and then either move on to further studies or land a good job. For the majority of young people currently in higher education, this is not the case.

So, what about us, poor 'soft subject' students? What are we to do when jobs are so hard to come by, when tuition fees have soared sky-high and the number of graduates exceeds the number of jobs tenfold if not more? What do you do to secure a good position that does not involve stacking shelves?

There is another challenge, too: humanities and creative arts students have relatively few contact hours with their lecturers and can really feel lost, not knowing what do with their time. I mean, come on, how many hours a day can you actually spend on studying? It is perfectly normal that students slip into procrastination and get carried away in a tempting whirlpool of mid-week parties. How do you deal with all those 'time holes' in your schedule?

The short answer to those questions is: use your time wisely to start developing your skills early. The long answer led me to writing this book. I have written it because I want to give you advice I wish I had been given in my first year. Advice that will make you employable and help you develop skills that all recruiters are looking for. Moreover, I promise that you will have a lot of fun in the process.

I am sorry for sounding like an infomercial – but this is what I'm offering here.

All students have to make effort in the current climate. More effort to get better grades, more effort to obtain the so-much-desired work experience, more effort to stand out and get noticed by the employers... but for the stigmatised students of the so-called 'soft subjects' the effort has to be double:

First of all, they have to fight for jobs just like everyone else;

Secondly, they have to fight the misconception and prejudice about the fact that they've chosen an 'easy option' (I will deal with these myths in **Chapter 5: A Kind Word about the 'Soft Subjects'**).

I am writing this to tell you how to:

- Make the most of your time at university;
- Gain work experience without ever leaving the campus;
- Acquire the skills that are essential at every workplace and present them on your CV with maximum effect (please see my book *How to Write a CV with Little or No Work Experience* that can be downloaded for FREE from *First Year Counts* and *The Lecture Room's* websites;
- Create a *community* of fans, friends, clients and supporters around you as a professional from the first days of the first year.

However, I must also warn you: there is no magic bullet. Nor will it be easy. Sorry for the cliché, but the only place where success comes before work is a dictionary. You will have to put in the work, because it's the only way to become outstanding. And that's what you want, right?

I suppose I speak too much about having a (corporate) job and becoming employable so that Mr. Big Boss likes you. Some of you might find this odd: after all, perhaps during the course of your studies you will realise you want to open your own company or even establish a charity after graduation. Or perhaps you will want to carry on studying and work in academia afterwards. Perhaps you want to be an artist, to be free and independent and have nothing to do with all those 'horrible corporate sour-faces'. You might think you do not need skills that a corporate employee needs.

I'm sorry, but I'll have to disappoint you again. When opening a business you become more than just a sole entrepreneur or an employer. You become your own employee, and there is nothing worse than opening your own company and having no skills that enhance your employability. You are working for yourself and if you don't know how to do your job well, you will lose everything. Opening a charity is the same as opening a business – except that profit is not a top priority. Yet, although filling your own pockets might not be as important, raising money and establishing meaningful business relationships will be paramount. Want to be an artist, a musician or a writer? Well, think about who will market you and put your products and services before your audience while you are still unknown! It will be you who does it, and no one else.

No, employability skills are everything. Sticking up your nose and saying that you have nothing in common with corporate employees is certainly not an option.

The same applies to working in academia. Although to you it might seem slightly removed from the real world, the academic world has never been more business, money and job-market oriented. Gone are the days when the world of academia was an 'ivory tower' full of eccentric folks with their minds somewhere out there. Education has become a big business and needs money in order to function effectively, giving students the best services (from lectures and seminars to bathrooms and internet connection).

So, whatever career you choose after graduating, employability has never been more important.

Some of the ideas you will find here never entered my head when I was an undergraduate. But, I suppose, it is the way of things: knowledge can only come with experience. I can tell you one thing for sure: I wish that back then I had had some of the ideas I am sharing with you now. I entered university when life looked bright. I managed without those tips for a year and a half, participating in the normal range of student activities: studying, having a part-time job in retail, sitting at the canal and playing my guitar, and partying from time to time.

It took me some time to realise that I shouldn't settle for silver when I could get gold. I started developing myself as a professional to get a work placement, to enhance my CV, and, eventually, to become an author entrepreneur by acquiring new skills through trial and error. But I could have started much earlier.

Your situation is different: you cannot afford the luxury of idleness. *You cannot afford starting later.* As soon as you arrive on campus you are in danger of becoming sucked in and overwhelmed. You've got to find ways to stand out from the crowd right away.

From the first day of the first year.

What is more, with the help of this book, you will find out how to enjoy it, too!

A few words about the cover image

The cover of *CAMP UK 10/2012* has been deliberately designed to show you what awaits you. On the one hand, you're just a student in a T-shirt; on the other, you're a soldier. The student is your exterior, the soldier – your spirit. I don't really like breaking it to you, but as soon as you step onto the campus, from the first days of the first year, you enter a state of war. And it is not war against your classmates or other graduates. It is war against your own stereotypes of university life. Prepare to be surprised. Prepare to be challenged. Prepare for a lot of positive change. Prepare to win the war!

15

For those who might be slightly shocked by my belligerent attitude, I repeat once again: your classmates are not your enemies. Think of the war as a game of paintball or capture-the-flag. You want to win – but you don't want to destroy everything around you in the process. However, you must have a strategy that works, you have to mobilise your resources and act boldly.

I don't promise it will be easy – but it will sure be worth it!

CHAPTER 3

WHY ARE YOU AT UNIVERSITY?

Each person's reasons for entering university are different. Yet, if we were to divide all students into groups according to what they are exactly doing at their institution, we would come up with four groups:

Group #1
Those who know exactly what they want from their courses

Most of them study vocational subjects like natural and life sciences, or number-based subjects like finance, engineering and computer science. Yet, it is not rare to see someone who studies humanities and social sciences in their midst – after all, there are people who want to be nothing else but teachers (perhaps even lecturers), social workers, archaeologists, translators and playwrights.

Yet, for all those who are doing a degree it is important to realise that your professional abilities are by no means limited by your degree. Someone with a degree in theology can become an IT consultant; a medicine graduate can become an actor or a singer-songwriter; an architect can open his or her own business that does not have to be related to architecture. There is nothing wrong with changing your career path and realising that your calling lies elsewhere.

Group #2
Those who know approximately what they want from their courses

They are studying a subject because they want to work in an area related to their studies. However, they have not yet decided where, exactly. For example, a biology student could become either a lab researcher, or a teacher, or an environmental officer; an English student could work in education, journalism, marketing and communications, or in publishing; a mathematics student can become an accountant or a software engineer.

Those people have more general skills and specialise less. They are more flexible and perhaps career transition is also easier for them due to this flexibility. They do not have a clearly defined career goal but they know where approximately they would like to work, and, more importantly, where they would not like to work at all.

Group #3
Those who are specialising in the subject they like

Some students are not sure what exactly they want to do as a career. They just want to study a subject they enjoy because they think that university should be not only about what one *must* do, but also about what one *likes* to do. There are more people like this among humanities and social sciences students. Their subjects are academic: philosophy, history, politics, languages and linguistics, cultural studies, sociology, etc.

Their time at university is the time of searching, trying and testing – they try to find out what they like; they try to find out what they are good at and what doesn't motivate them that much.

There is absolutely nothing wrong with that. I must say that when those people become serious about what they are doing, they can reach enormous success – because one of the essential components of success is enjoying what you're doing. But it takes some courage to make that final leap towards becoming serious. I hope that, having read this book, you will make that leap.

Group #4
Those who have been tricked into believing that going to university alone will land them a well-paid job and a great skyrocketing career

These people go to university 'to have better job prospects' – often without any other, more specific goals in mind. They do have a bit of the other three groups in them. On the whole, it is great that they do take initiative and try to enhance their chances of employment by continuing their education. What is not so great, however, is that they often let the university life just happen to them, waiting to graduate and be offered a job on a platter.

The bitter truth is that they do not realise that the world does not work like this anymore. If one merely does a degree without giving himself/herself a good account of what they are doing, golden opportunities can be missed. As I already said above, everyone is a graduate nowadays. Many have good degree classifications. Many have work experience. Those to whom university 'just happens' do not stand a chance.

I want *you* to become the guys and girls from Group Number One.

It is important to understand very clearly what you want from your university experience, both personally and professionally – and then claim it. You have to go for it and everything you do every day must contribute to that goal. You have to understand very clearly what you've got yourself involved in when you accepted that degree course offer.

I repeat: as soon as you step onto the campus, you enter a state of war. But this war is like nothing you've seen before. It is a war whose rules are so twisted that it might make your head spin.

But before we begin discussing the rules, let me tell you what you are offered when you enter university. In other words, what you're paying for. I want to do this now, in the beginning, so that you can start making plans regarding the best use of your time here.

CHAPTER 4

WHAT DOES UNIVERSITY REALLY OFFER YOU?

I have to admit and acknowledge that being a fresher is not easy. Many of you are away from home for the first time. You have to adapt to your new life: living alone, living away from your family, managing the studying, the cooking, the shopping, the cleaning and the partying all by yourself. Independent life can be very hectic and difficult sometimes, and lecture material as well as homework can also be tough. Yet, your independent life has some enormous advantages, too. Finally, you've got a lot of time for yourself – and you can use that time to develop new skills, and those skills can extend way beyond writing an essay on the last day before the submission or crash-courses in smart exam revision. They can extend beyond learning to dance salsa, making delicious budget meals and living off your last cash before you are overdrawn.

I am talking about skills for life and for success. Skills that will make you employable and help you stand out.

I am sorry for sounding like an infomercial *again*, but I'm just telling you the truth. This book is about what chances university offers you and how to take advantage of them. For your tuition fees, university offers you a lot more than meets the eye. Besides the usual educational programme that involves the lecturers passing on their knowledge and then testing if you've been paying attention, university offers a lot of other things. They are there for you – but you have to go after them with a club. Sometimes you've got to work harder to find

21

opportunities to develop yourself – but you will always find them if you seek them.

So, here is what university offers you for your tuition fees:

1. Lectures, labs and seminars (obviously)

2. Testing and evaluation of your knowledge (duh!)

3. Opportunities to establish professional relations with your lecturers. After all, lecturers exist not only to stand in front of you and talk. They are there to help you – and it pays off to establish good relations with them. First of all, you can talk to your lecturers about any concerns you might have about your studies. Secondly, your lecturers are most likely to be the first people to provide you with a reference – so make sure they have a lot of great stuff to write about you!

4. Access to the library – both physical and electronic. The electronic library is especially important for assignment writing. Many students turn to academic books (or just course textbooks) when writing their essays; yet, they often miss out on academic journals that contain much more interesting and in-depth information than books. Most academic journals that universities subscribe to are kept in electronic format and checking out e-libraries as well as Google Scholar (http://scholar.google.com) is definitely worth it, especially if you want to deepen your knowledge and show your lecturer that you approach your assignments seriously. You can find more information about academic development on the websites I have already mentioned (*The Lecture Room* and *First Year Counts*), as well as in my book *From Confusion to Conclusion: How to Write a First Class Essay*.

5. On-campus internet. This may not seem much to you at first, but I think you will change your mind when you read **Chapter 12: Students and online presence**. In it, I explain that internet in university can be used for much more than checking your email and Facebook. Internet offers you enormous possibilities, and you should make good use of them all. Read **Chapters 12 and 13** to find out more.

6. Access to student clubs and societies. Usually you've got to pay a membership fee (about a fiver for an ordinary society; could be more for specialised sports clubs like martial arts), but it's not a lot compared to what being a member of a society can offer you. More information can be found in **Chapter 9: On Hiring Yourself (Get Involved)**.

7. Access to on-campus student jobs. A bit of extra cash as well as work experience is always handy. From the local pub to the university library, there are plenty of opportunities to find paid work. Many universities have their own job centres, too! You can find more information on student employment and work experience in **Chapter 8: How to Get Awesome Work Experience While You Are Still at University**.

8. A special status in society. If you're out of school, you are just another jobseeker. If you're a graduate who has not learnt how to be outstanding, you are just another jobseeker as well. However, if you are a student, people view you differently. You have a purpose, a reason to be in a certain place, a reason to look for work, and people think of you as a person who aims higher. It's a great reputation to have – so do not ruin it!

And finally, stemming from all the above, university offers you the following:

9. Opportunities to get work experience beyond the usual range of 'student jobs'

10. Opportunities to develop the most important skills for work and life: communication, teamwork, interpersonal, research and analysis, problem-solving – and, in fact, any professional skills for any occupation you desire

11. Opportunities to become a professional from the first day of the first year

12. Opportunities to stand out from the general pool of graduates and to become remarkable

Read on to find out how you can do it!

CHAPTER 5

A KIND WORD ABOUT THE 'SOFT SUBJECTS'

NB: If you do study arts, humanities, social sciences (this includes business) or any other subject I mentioned in Chapter 2, please read this chapter carefully. If you happen to study a science or mathematics-related subject and happen to look down upon those who have elected 'the soft option', please read this chapter carefully, twice.

Several years ago I had a conversation with an elderly gentleman in the middle of Birmingham. I don't remember how the conversation turned to my education, but the gentleman asked what I wanted to do with my life after university.

At that time, I had neither the courage to say I was going to be a writer, nor the discipline to write every day that would justify my choice of profession. So I said:

'I hope to work in research, in university or a think-tank.'

It wasn't entirely a lie – of all full-time jobs, research-related ones seemed the most appealing and the most interesting to me.

'What, get paid for thinking?' the man replied with a hint of irony in his voice. 'What the world needs are more engineers and brain surgeons!'

I agreed with him then and I still do. Yet, I am neither an engineer nor a brain surgeon. I hold a First in International Relations and English. Having studied an academic, nonvocational subject, should I be considered less valuable as an employee because of that? I don't think so. Let me explain why.

If we think seriously, what does a degree give you? A piece of paper that shows you know something? The paper, yes; I am not so sure about the knowledge, though. An advantage when looking for a better-paid job? Perhaps, but I would not count on that. Someone without a degree who has got several years of work experience can also be hired for the same skilled job. Lack of a degree does not equal lack of intelligence. Skills for doing certain jobs well? Yes, this one is a closer shot. A good vocational degree like pharmacy or engineering will indeed equip you with professional skills. But are these skills alone a guarantee of a good graduate position? Unfortunately, they are not.

A degree in the so-called 'soft subjects' can teach you to think. It can teach you not to believe one opinion but always check if that opinion can be backed up by facts. You will also learn that there can be more than one point of view (after all, even theories like the Big Bang or the Evolution are not absolute truths – they are just theories that are used by scientists because they explain some things in a way scientists like). It will teach you to read – because reading is a skill that must be learnt not only in primary school. People must continue to learn to read all their lives and 'soft' degrees will teach you to read a text, an event, a painting, a historical source, a pattern of human behaviour and trends in social movements. You will be taught to search for information in a clever manner and not to believe everything you read. You will also be taught some subject-specific skills which will depend on your degree choice. You will be taught to appreciate the beauty of human thought and countless forms of its expression.

But you will not be taught how to find a job. You will not be taught how to become employable.

In fact, even degrees like law or finance will not teach you how to get a job either, nor can they guarantee you will get one.

There is one general truth you must realise about university degrees. No degree – be it finance, IT, medicine, media studies, foreign languages or history of art – will ever benefit you unless you take it seriously.

There are no non-serious subjects in university – there are only non-serious approaches.

In other words, your degree – in fact, your entire university experience – is only what you decide to make of it. Everything depends on you. This thought is encouraging because no one should be able to question the value of your education, but it's also unsettling, because it puts the entire burden of responsibility for your employability on your shoulders.

Going back to my four groups of students (see **Chapter 3**), I must say that there are a lot of people in arts, humanities and social sciences who may enjoy the subject they indulge in just enough to make some real effort in classes, but they still lack determination to take their university life and their degree seriously. This prevents them from succeeding even if they like what they are doing.

In other words, they are not aware that university is a boot camp which has been already touched by the war (or that the paintball match is in full swing, if you like). They do not know they are supposed to fight for every opportunity to become better – and that the opportunities are out there for them, at arm's reach.

When I talk about my degree, I talk about it in two ways. First of all, I mention what it has *given* to me. Next, I tell what I *have taken* from it. Those things are not the same. What a degree (and your university) gives you is a limited number of items, handed to you on a golden platter. What you take from it is a great number of awesome things, but you have to go for them, armed with a big bad machine gun of determination. Your time at university can offer many experiences of which you are probably unaware.

I began taking what rightfully belonged to me rather late. However, when I gave myself a kick in the backside and took hold of my own success, my entire world turned upside-down... But I'm rushing too much with the story. Let's talk about everything in the right order.

CHAPTER 6

HOW I REALISED WHAT I WANTED FROM LIFE. AND THEN HOW I DID IT AGAIN. AND AGAIN

When I came to university, initially, I had chosen to study business. Even when enrolling, I knew it would not be what I like doing. Yet, for some stupid reason, I believed that my education should be practical. I did not want to 'indulge in a soft subject'. I had naively believed that one needs a 'practical' degree to get a good job – I didn't know several things back then.

I didn't know that a 'serious-sounding' degree title means nothing when you are looking for a job;

I didn't know that for most 'office' jobs it doesn't matter what degree course you have studied;

I didn't know that it's not a 'serious' degree that matters, but a serious attitude;

I didn't know that in order to succeed at something, one must enjoy it;

But then, I was a different person, too.

I was living a 'usual' student life. I did have a part-time job as a sales assistant that paid my bills. I was studying business administration, trying to be good at everything and even succeeding. I had good grades for mathematics and economics – not because I liked them but because I was trained to do well since the early days of school. I finished my first year with a

70% average grade and everything should have been good for me.

Except that it wasn't.

Towards the second term of the first year I realised that I did not enjoy what I was doing at all. I had been lying to myself, and I was able do that for a year, but no longer. Then I decided that I had two choices: either to stay where I was and continue leading an unhappy and reclusive life, or to make a decision that took real courage and start doing something I truly enjoyed.

Changing my course was not easy.

Few people understood the motivation behind my decision.

I was attending a business studies course at a university with a great business school. I had a first class average grade for the first year. And yet, I decided to quit my course and study international relations and English. Why?

Many of my friends thought I was making the most irrational decision in my life. They said:

'No matter what you want to be in life, you should know how business operates. So, stick to what you're doing, grit your teeth and get through it!'

They were right about the first part: I had to learn how business operates. I am still learning it because being an author entrepreneur means living in a very competitive business setting. But I am learning it in a user-friendly environment, with no pressure on me. I am learning it because I want to.

But back then, every cell of my body screamed in protest. My brain refused to process lecture material. I felt I was out of place. I did not belong in the business studies programme, no matter how good it was. I could not pretend I liked it any longer – and I could not do something for which I had no enthusiasm.

Taking the decision to change my degree course was difficult. There were several reasons why:

1. I was an overseas student.

Most of my compatriots were studying in the business school, with some others in the school of engineering. All of them were 'showing they were serious about life because they were studying a "serious" subject'. International students do not study 'soft' subjects – this statistical fact turned into a public opinion that I had to counter, at least in my own mind.

2. The stigma attached to 'soft' subjects.

Usually subjects like arts, humanities, languages and social sciences are regarded as 'easy' and 'a soft option'. I had to go against the current and prove the opposite (see my reflections on it in the previous chapter).

3. I already owed the Student Loans Company.

One year of studies had been already paid for. I could not jump straight into the second year and had to start my course anew, from year one. This meant getting into more debt.

However, I did it. And if I had not done it, this book would have probably never been written.

It was only after making the change that I started following the advice that I am giving here. Because I was finally doing something in which I believed.

Moreover, I had a clear idea where I was heading. I had a goal, a purpose that fulfilled me both professionally and personally. I loved linguistics and I wanted to work in the field. Then I turned a little more business-like and landed a placement in communications, before going back to creative writing and non-fiction. My goals changed with time, the professional direction of my life shifted, but as I progressed through my studies and work, I realised more and more clearly what I really wanted from my studies, from my work and from my life.

I have always wanted to be a writer. And not just a grumpy solitary one who spends hours upon hours at his typewriter and then silently hands his manuscript to the publisher. I wanted to be someone who inspires others, who can share his experiences and valuable information with others. Now I am here, doing that.

I achieved my goals for two simple reasons:

- I liked what I was doing and therefore was motivated to succeed at it;
- I realised that a serious degree course is nothing; a serious approach to your work is everything.

I did change my professional plans several times – perhaps sometimes I wanted to take many avenues at once to be safe and then discard some choices when certain doors closed. I wanted to get a placement in public relations, and I achieved this goal (you can read about it in **Chapter 9**, under the section called *How I Got a Work Placement in the Middle of the Recession*). Then I wanted to prove myself as an academic researcher and I got that, too: I published three papers and presented at conferences whilst still being an undergraduate; I wanted to try myself in translation and I got an internship in the EU thanks to the skills I have obtained during my university studies. Finally, I decided that, all this time, I wanted to be a writer, which has led me to writing this book as well as three others – one on creating a CV when you have little or no work experience and the other two on writing successful academic essays and dissertations. Here's the (incomplete) list of the outcomes of my course change:

1. A first class degree with a prize for academic achievement
2. A work placement as Communications Officer in a science research council
3. A wealth of experience in marketing, promotional work, communications and writing, all of which has led to me becoming an author entrepreneur

4. Three years' work experience as a writing mentor in the university library (teaching people essay writing skills). I wanted to share my knowledge and experience with others and wrote two books: *From Confusion to Conclusion: How to Write a First Class Essay* and *How -to Write a First-Class Dissertation* (the latter one is targeted at final-year students). Some chapters of the books as well as other great FREE content can be downloaded at www.FirstYearCounts.com and

   www.TheLectureRoom.co.uk

5. Runner-up in a student essay competition thanks to my passion for what I was studying

6. Three academic papers and two conference presentations in the field of linguistics while I was still an undergraduate. Anyone who is interested in publishing their undergraduate research, please see **Chapter 11**

7. Three short stories published in a small literary magazine

8. A FREE eBook called *How to Write a CV with Little or No Work Experience* published online, summing up my professional experience

   The entire eBook can be downloaded for FREE when you subscribe to the newsletter on www.TheLectureRoom.co.uk and

   www.FirstYearCounts.com

9. And finally – following my goals and becoming an author entrepreneur with dozens of ideas how to help others succeed.

I don't know what you will make of this list, but to me this looks like I've got quite a lot done during university. And the best news is that if I could do it, you can do it, too. Of course, there's no need to repeat my path – carve your own and have fun in the process!

CHAPTER 7

THE ONLY TWO STEPS TOWARDS SUCCESS YOU WILL EVER NEED TO TAKE

In this chapter, I will talk about becoming successful.

Everyone defines (professional) success in their own way. For some, success means a well-paid job and quick cash to buy a house (or several). For others, success is a job that pays just about enough, but which they thoroughly enjoy and that brings pleasure. Some define success as getting paid for one's hobby. For some, success is doing a job they find meaningful – for example, through being able to help people in need. It does not matter what definition of success you use. All I want to do is share some advice on how to achieve it, starting from the first days of your first year.

In order to become successful at university, you need two very simple things: *to get involved and to be seen*.

The rest of this book will tell you exactly how to do it. So, what exactly do I mean?

Getting Involved in extracurricular activities is the key to getting work experience at university. In plain English, it means that you will have to spend a lot of time doing stuff. This means joining student societies for *active* membership; it also means volunteering to help your university as much as you can by becoming a course representative or getting involved in university management (I will talk about it in detail in

Chapter 8: How to Get Awesome Work Experience at University).

Being seen is paramount in the modern world if you want to succeed. A crowd of graduates is exactly what it looks like – a crowd. Moreover, it is a very noisy crowd where everyone roars: *Hire me! Hey, Mr. Big Boss, look over here! I'm here, educated, talented, a real problem solver, motivated! Hire me! Buy my talent!*

So, how do you get heard in a crowd where everyone shouts?

The answer is: don't shout.

Your voice will never be heard in a crowd because you cannot shout louder than those thousands of people. What you can do, however, is talk to ONE person.

However, there is one condition, which is absolutely necessary for that person to start listening to you. They have to know you and think you are worth listening to.

In other words, you have to be famous with them. Famous in a small circle. More importantly, *famous on the internet*.

In the modern world, when it comes to employment and making money, either by having a full-time job or by managing your own business, there is only one sure way to become famous: get online and do something useful, free of charge.

Yes, you heard me right. You have to become unselfish in order to achieve greatness. Because this is why you picked up this book in the first place, right?

Now, all of this might seem a bit confusing to you at the start, but I will explain everything in **Chapter 12: Students and Online Presence** and **Chapter 13: A Short Blogging Course**. When you reach those chapters, I ask you to read them carefully. They contain information university is not likely to teach you.

The next chapter will tell you how to get work experience.

CHAPTER 8

HOW TO GET AWESOME WORK EXPERIENCE AT UNIVERSITY

University is much more than your course of study. One of the most fascinating secrets about university is that it is a perfect place for getting invaluable work experience.

So, let's start from the basics. There are five main ways to get work experience while you are a student:

1. Having a standard part-time student job

2. Doing paid and unpaid internships

3. Volunteering inside and outside university

4. Becoming a freelancer

and, most importantly,

5. *Hiring yourself and becoming responsible for your own fate*.

The fifth point is what this book is all about. However, for now let's talk about all the points in greater detail. I will describe each of them and assess its advantages and drawbacks. Let's go!

8.1. Having a Part-Time Student Job

If you happen to hold one of those, consider yourself lucky. This means that your university is situated in a town or city large enough to need part-time workforce. One of the easiest ways to get a part-time student job is to ask around the campus – more often than not, universities employ their own students. Here's a list of jobs you can do without even leaving the campus:

- Catering (kitchen work, washing dishes, serving tables, etc.)
- Pub work (bartender, waitress, etc.)
- Campus shops (bookstore, stationer shop, food outlets, etc.)
- Cleaning/Housekeeping (forget about it being 'prestigious' or not – a job is a job)
- Casual administrative work (e.g. stuffing envelopes – just ask around the busy offices; moreover, jobs like these are often advertised by email)
- Library work (shelving, etc.); also seasonal, but they often need help
- Mentoring (this is not so common, but sometimes university libraries do take student tutors, especially if they are exceptionally good with figures and can help their fellow students with maths; some universities also have academic writing mentors – I've worked as one for three years)
- Student ambassadors (those jobs are fairly common; you tell school kids and sixth formers how many terrific opportunities university offers as well as performing other tasks, e.g., administrative)
- Promotional work (e.g. leaflet distribution and becoming a 'brand ambassador')

Of course, this list is far from exhaustive. Those opportunities do differ from university to university. They are all great, for several reasons. First of all, they pay your bills – and this is one of the main concerns for students. Secondly, they give you some work experience. It is not true that to gain those transferable skills, which everyone says modern graduates lack, you need to hold an office job. Things like motivation, teamwork, working on your own initiative and commercial awareness can be learnt in a pub or in a team of hotel porters. There is a lot you can talk about during an interview or write in your application form: managing conflicts, co-operating with the rest of the team to achieve a particular goal, effective communication, taking initiative etc. Employers do not demand office experience because they understand it is hard to get when one is an undergraduate.

Yet, no matter how proud you might be of your achievements in a particular job, it still is nothing but a student job. You have responsibilities, yet, let's face it: your initiatives are largely the result of the boss breathing down your neck.

If you want to achieve something truly remarkable, you should take initiative by yourself. You should do something because you want to create value – and not just for your boss who will praise you. I will talk more about it in Section 8.5. For now, let's move to the next work experience opportunity.

8.2. Placements and Internships

Of course, those are a little harder to get than a normal student job. You need to find ways to present your limited experience in a way that will convince your future employer that your every achievement is worthy of a Nobel Prize. You can read about this in my eBook *How to Write a CV with Little or No Work Experience* which you can download for free either from *The Lecture Room* or *First Year Counts.*

Internships have one great disadvantage: they are scarce and competition for them can be enormous. Let's admit it: not everyone will get them. Moreover, internships are offered in a limited number of fields. They are all rather mainstream: business-related (accounting, finance, human resources, etc.); engineering of all sorts (mechanical, electric, software, etc.); media and publishing in large corporations; research and analysis of different kinds. If you want to work in a more 'exotic' area, such as creative arts or education, placements and internships are much rarer and harder to get.

Naturally, if an internship is either paid, or very prestigious, or both, there will be a lot of competition. One of the ways to beat competition is volunteering. The next section is all about it.

8.3. Volunteering

Broadly speaking, volunteering means giving your time and effort to work with a charity or a non-profit organisation so that your work benefits the wider community.

Volunteering can benefit you in several ways. First of all, being only an undergraduate *you can get a job that you normally wouldn't* – that's why it is so important to you, as a student. You can work as a PR officer, a charity fundraiser, an editor, an actor/actress, a photographer, a social worker, a journalist for a serious website, an environmental officer, a music production engineer or an events manager... You can also work in art and design-related fields. The opportunities are endless. Volunteering can be a great way to get ahead for people of creative professions.

Secondly, your future employer will be only too pleased to see that you've freely given something you cannot get back – your time and effort. Managers like to see that you've invested in yourself, learnt new skills and contributed to a greater cause. *It looks great on your CV.*

Thirdly, you get to meet new interesting people and develop a sense of achievement, of meaningful work that benefits not only you but also someone else. Volunteering changes lives – including that of the volunteer – and there is a lot to be learnt from it.

There are two types of voluntary work available for students: in the university and outside it. The number of opportunities depends on the size of the town you are living in. Almost every university has a volunteer centre. It is definitely worth visiting them to find out what opportunities there are. Here are the key areas in which people normally volunteer:

- Children and young people
- Vulnerable adults
- Health
- Conservation and the environment
- Arts, culture and media
- Sports and leisure

Another place to volunteer is your own student union: you could join a committee or a steering group and have a say in the way your own university is run. You could also run for student officer elections. If you have ideas that could help make university a better experience for students, do not hesitate to become active!

There is also another, more exotic way to volunteer and make a difference, increasingly popular nowadays: going to a Third World country and working for a specific amount of time to benefit the local community. Usually British students build schools or medical and sanitary facilities, teach English and work on various other community projects. These opportunities are invaluable because the exposure to other cultures and ways of looking at the world can actually change *your* life. They teach you how rewarding such work can be, equip you with a great number of skills necessary for employment and give you something outstanding to talk about at a job interview. However, not everyone can afford such experience – in terms of time or money. Not everyone is free of family commitments. Not everyone can go and do some charitable work in a foreign country because there are communities next door that also need help. It's popular, but not mainstream.

When it comes to volunteering 'at home', universities are usually connected to volunteering schemes that exist nationwide, so you could find that activities inside and outside university overlap quite a lot. Check out these links for volunteering in the United Kingdom:

http://www.volunteering.org.uk/

www.do-it.org.uk

http://www.csv.org.uk/volunteering

There is one important thing you need to remember when looking for volunteering opportunities: there is always something for you. Even if the area in which you would like to volunteer is not advertised, you MUST go and ask around. Whether you'd like to volunteer in a museum or in a theatre, or even with the police... all you have to do is go and inquire. If they say no, do not give up. Be persistent. Sometimes the reason you get a 'no' is because you talk to a wrong person who is just too busy or does not like making additional effort. Do not give up and keep asking around.

8.4. Becoming a Freelancer

If you feel you've got some skills that you could sell, it's worth looking into freelancing opportunities. Being a self-employed freelancer can have many benefits. You are in charge of your own schedule, have an opportunity to work from home and still gain and develop an impressive set of skills to put on your CV that will make employers interested in you. First of all, you develop your entrepreneurial skills because being a freelancer is the same as having your own business. You must find an opportunity to apply your skills, gradually build a great reputation and thus increase the number of clients. What is more, you develop outstanding self-motivation because your work depends entirely on your initiative. Here are some things you can do as a student:

Teaching

Become a freelance tutor. Put up an advert on the wall in your university, advertising your skills:

- Languages (including English as a second language)
- Maths (especially in demand; pretty profitable, too!)
- IT
- Science
- Practically, anything else you want, from graphic design to fine pottery

You can also go to a few local schools and put up your advert there. There will always be people who need some additional mentoring – and they (or their parents) will be ready to pay you for your efforts.

Also, for tutoring in the UK, visit these sites:

http://www.uktutors.com/
http://www.localtutor.co.uk/Tuition_Information/
UK_Tutors.html
http://www.firsttutors.com/uk/

You can register on those sites for free and advertise your services as a freelance tutor in any field from art design to zoology, as well as set your rates. I advise you to be competitive and not charge too much – after all, you are only an undergraduate student, not a PhD graduate with 10 years of experience. See how much others charge for their services and charge a slightly lower price. Do not make it too low, either – we don't want everyone to lower their prices in a hectic 'race to the bottom'.

Translation and interpreting

Speak another language at native level and have good communication skills? Try freelance translation and interpreting. Just find out email addresses of as many agencies as you can, and apply to all of them. Even as a student, you can get plenty of work and use your language skills. It is also a highly rewarding job: after all you're helping people communicate! Yet, it can be rather tough, too – I have worked as a freelance public service interpreter and on several occasions I've had to interpret for asylum seekers in solicitors' offices as well as in HM prisons. I must say that the experience was rather emotionally draining. Female interpreters can get jobs at maternity hospitals and abortion clinics. One must have a certain mindset to work in those areas – but if you're up for it, then it's an excellent chance to hone your language skills and earn some cash in the process.

Other freelance projects

If you have certain abilities, teaching is not your only option – you might want to work according to those abilities. There are many websites through which you can find, and bid for, freelance projects. Here are some examples of what you can do:

- Website design
- Writing, proofreading and editing
- Transcribing (typing words from audio recordings)
- Graphic design
- Translation
- Computer programming

There is one problem with doing freelance work – when you are an undergraduate student people tend to regard you as unreliable. In order for people to take you more seriously, you need to have a solid portfolio of works, some testimonies and experience. Naturally, in the beginning these are hard to get – but if you are ready to grit your teeth and work hard for your goals, you can build yourself as a professional by your final year. It takes time to build a serious portfolio, but, should you decide to pursue freelancing further, it is really worth it.

In the next chapters, I will talk about how to build a portfolio that showcases your best work. I would like to note, however, that every professional – not only freelancers, but also those in full time employment – must have a portfolio of best works, so making the effort to do this now can only be an advantage to you later.

8.5. Hiring Yourself and Becoming Responsible for Your Own Fate

This point may seem a bit strange and hard to understand at first. Let me clarify it.

What do I mean by 'hiring yourself'? Every student wants to be a graduate and eventually become a professional in one area or another. Every student wants to be employable and be hired – and it doesn't matter what job you want to do in the future. Being a corporate lawyer involves being hired as much as does being a charity worker, a rock singer or even a writer. There is always a person on whom a professional depends: formal employees with permanent contracts depend on their bosses; freelance graphic designers depend on their customers; rock singers depend on their listeners; writers depend on their editors and readers (more on the latter, actually, because an editor can reject a good book but a reader will never do it).

Those are the people who hire you, who are willing to pay for your talent, invest in your potential and gain something out of it.

However, there is one enormous mistake that the majority of students make. They wait till their graduation to be hired. They do not have the experience of what it really means to be **hired**.

Even those who do have part-time jobs, or even manage to land fancy internships in companies with loud names, sometimes don't know what it really means to be hired.

How can this be? What do I mean? What does it mean to be hired, then?

Being hired means being made responsible for something. Even simplest, unskilled jobs involve a degree of responsibility. However, when it comes to the work opportunities at university that I have mentioned above, the first three (part-time student jobs, internships, and volunteering) involve being accountable to someone. There is always a boss over you. There is always someone who regulates your actions. Therefore, sometimes your job, however, wonderful, can restrict the number of skills you can learn.

For example, in some jobs you work on your own. Those kinds of jobs do help you improve your self-motivation and encourage you to take initiative, but they don't help you develop your teamwork skills at all (good examples of those types of jobs are cold-calling, street fundraising or even housekeeping). Other jobs help you enhance your research skills, but may teach you nothing about commercial awareness. In short, one job, or one type of activity cannot teach you everything.

When it comes to self-employment, you have more freedom to regulate your own activities and learn more skills that make you employable. However, you have the biggest freedom to develop yourself as a professional when you decide to *hire yourself* – in other words, when you start doing something that places all responsibility for the process, the outcomes, and the skills you will learn into your own hands.

This is also the most difficult path: you are not accountable to anyone but yourself. It can be hard to find the strength to do all those things at once and juggle your studies with a part-time job and all those activities that help you gain important skills. However, there is no other way. You have to learn to juggle them – and that is why it is vital that you start from the first day of the first year, while the global panic about decimal points of the average grade has not yet gripped you by the throat.

In this book, getting hired means becoming responsible first and foremost to yourself. Even when you work for someone else, you must ask yourself the following questions: What am I doing here? Am I doing this job well? How much can I learn at this job? What can I do to learn more? How much more can I learn here?

However, once you understand that you are not only an employee, but also the boss; once you take your future into your hands and have the freedom to develop yourself in whichever direction, those questions start burning your mind with intensity you have not experienced before.

So, how do you *hire yourself*? As always, here's the list of what you need to do:

1. Take things seriously;
2. Decide what you like and what you want;
3. Become active;
4. Become well-known with a narrow audience;
5. Become **unselfish**.

In the following chapters, I will explain what I mean by each of these.

CHAPTER 9

ON HIRING YOURSELF (GET INVOLVED)

There is a reason why I repeat certain things in this book – and it's not because I want to increase the word count like I would when writing an academic essay with a very tight deadline. You are my audience, you are all extremely busy people, and I respect your time. The reason why I repeat things is because I want certain truths to really sink in.

Here's another one of those truths: **consider yourself lucky just because you are at university**.

I can tell you for sure that under no other circumstances would you be able to get so many opportunities for development. As I have already pointed out, there are five steps to success and employability. In this chapter, I am going to introduce you to the first three: taking things seriously, deciding what you want and what you like, and becoming active. I will leave the other two – becoming famous with a small audience and becoming unselfish – for later. Let's start.

9.1. Take Things Seriously

As it was already pointed out in Chapter 4, there is no such thing as a 'serious' or 'non-serious' degree course. The only thing that matters is your attitude and your approach.

So, why are you doing your course? What's your approach like? You want to make money out of a good job in the future? Good. You like your subject and have an academic interest in it?

Even better! You know more or less what you want to do with your life? You want to work in a meaningful job that makes a difference? Excellent!

But what exactly are you willing to do to make your university experience a success? How much time and effort are you going to invest into your studies? What about extra-curricular activities? And don't forget about additional learning (reading, attending events and talking to people who can help you achieve your objectives) that is not compulsory but would really benefit you both academically and professionally.

How much are you willing to put in? If you want to get the most out of your time at university, prepare to have much less free time and work harder. Many people who criticise the modern university system say that young people go to university for the experience rather than for their academic degree. It may be partly true, but your university experience is also what you decide you want it to be – it can include nothing but fun and partying, but it can also be fun and skill-developing, it can include fun and active involvement in student societies, and investing in your future. You can take that university experience seriously, and this is when you become truly unstoppable!

9.2. Decide What You Like and What You Want

This does sound somewhat banal and clichéd. However, there is no point in delving into your degree course and starting actively obtaining valuable skills if you do not have a goal, if you don't know where all your efforts are leading.

Naturally, when you're in your first year, it is hard to know what you want to do professionally in the future. You might discover the passion of your life only several years later. You might work in one area for quite a time before you realise you want something completely different.

So, what do you do now, when you're young and, possibly, unsure?

First for all, you need to think what you like doing. This is simple – you *know* what you like. All you need to do is look back and think about what you've enjoyed the most over the course of the past several years. It might be your hobby, or a sport, or any activity. For the purposes of now, it is fine even if that interest has no potential to become a profession.

Secondly, you need to think what you want to do professionally. A frequent reply to words like these is: but I haven't even done my degree yet! I need to study, then work here and there, and only then decide what I want.

This is not true. Of course, getting a job and some work experience is one of the ways of finding out what you are good at, what tasks you can perform naturally and which ones are not so easy. However, it is definitely not the only way. In order to understand what you want professionally, you do not need to look forward – you need to look back. Review your recent past. Think what you have always enjoyed most. What subjects were your favourites at school? What did you study at sixth form? What elements of those subjects did you enjoy most? What did you do in your spare time? What kinds of people do you like meeting? What kinds of tasks do you like doing?

After you understand what you like and what you want, start looking for opportunities to develop your academic, professional, and employability-transferable skills by doing something you like and enjoy. This is where the third part – getting involved – comes in.

9.3. Become Active. Get Involved in Student societies

I am sure you all have heard about student societies. They are social groups, or clubs, based around something their members have in common – a hobby, a sport, being from a certain country or having an interest in one, speaking a certain language, etc. When you are at university, especially in your first year, being a member of a student society is an excellent opportunity to gain work experience.

As you probably know, every society has an executive committee: a president, a vice-president, a treasurer, and a secretary. Of course, when you are in your first year, those positions are occupied by someone who ran for election the previous academic year. However, if you do wish to have a position of responsibility next year, you, too, can run for elections and perhaps become an executive member. This looks great on your CV and provides you with a real challenge, testing your management, organisational and team-working skills.

But let me ask you something: what does the word 'President' on your CV really mean?

The correct answer is: 'nothing'. It is only a word and nothing more.

In my view, going for a position of power is nice, but what is much more important is not the position you occupy but the things you do, even if you do not hold that position.

Why run for presidency or vice-presidency? To have that word on your CV? Your CV is not about the position but about the achievements – and you can become active in a society without your post pressing you to do so. I must say that employers like it, too – such behaviour shows your entrepreneurial spirit, can-do attitude and willingness to take initiative without being asked.

So, let's discuss how you can use membership in a student society to your advantage:

1. Find a society you like and join it.

I will repeat this several times in the book because in my view it is one of the most important things you must realise: *you can only achieve true success if you like what you're doing*. Even though you have to work hard, I am begging you not to do anything that makes you feel like you have no place there. There is no need to join the Barbecue Society if you're vegetarian. Membership in the French Society is no use for you if you are studying Spanish and are not planning to learn French (although university is also the best place to learn a foreign language – see more about learning vital skills in **Chapter 10: Skills all Employers Require and Where to Get Them**). A finance society will not help you if you have no willingness to study maths or do a job that involves dealing with figures all day. In short, your society must either suit your goals or correspond to your interests. We are talking about gaining skills for employment and you can obtain them by doing what you like and feel strongly about.

2. If you can't find a society you like, establish one!

Now, this is a bit more difficult. Usually universities have societies for every taste – from standard sports clubs like football or karate to more exotic interest-based societies like Extreme Ironing or even Quidditch. However, if your university really does not have a society to your liking, then you can use your organisational skills, find several like-minded people and establish a society of your own.

Just remember that it's easy to open one but much harder to maintain it open and active – just like with a start-up company. You will have to spend a lot of time organising activities, you will need a lot of help in the beginning, but it's definitely a worthwhile experience. Starting your own society is like starting a business – the roots are bitter but the fruits are sweet.

3. Become active in that society.

Many students join societies to selfishly benefit from the membership: they participate in the events that others organise; they come to enjoy the atmosphere that took a lot of time and effort to create; they think that a society exists on its own, without realising how much work every gathering involves.

In other words, those people are consumers. Sadly, they are the majority.

There is one thing I want you to understand about consumers: they are passive. They enjoy the fruits of the others' labour; they do not pull their weight in a society; most importantly, they miss out on a great chance to develop employability skills for their future.

I want you to stop being a consumer and start being a value creator. What really matters is your involvement in the life of your society. You need to become active and get involved as much as you can – and you have to do it from the first days of the first year.

Here's how you can do it:

Help organise events

I can bet that your executive committee organises quite a few events for the society. Those can be sporting competitions, social gatherings like going bowling or paintballing together, charity sales, trips around the country for fun or for business, or even serious learning events like seminars, training and trips to conferences.

I can assure you of one thing – the executive committee are working their backsides off to make it good and if you offer your help, they will only appreciate it. Forget that you don't hold a position of responsibility. Just offer a helping hand and you will be given things to be responsible for and learn some skills in the process.

A great way to get some organisational experience is to take initiative and plan a small event yourself. Naturally, there is no need to work alone – engage with the society, tell them about your ideas. They will help you find the venue. Then talk to your university events officer – he or she will help you with publicising the event. If you ask the media department nicely, and if they are not too busy, they might even create a poster for you! Talk to people – most of the time they are willing to help.

Organising an event can teach you a lot about the state of your current skills and help you improve them – so think of something interesting and implement it!

Share useful information

Send around news and other interesting items (articles, videos, podcasts, etc.) that could be relevant to the members of the society. Gain the reputation of a person who knows a lot of useful stuff.

The best way to do it is through a Facebook page or group. It is even better if your society has a blog. I will talk about this later in **Chapters 12 and 13**, where I will explain how to create great online visibility for yourself as a professional, and how this can raise your profile in the eyes of all the people you are going to work with in the future.

Take members to events

First of all, research all events that you think your society members would like to attend. *Eventbrite* is a good website to start with. Next, select those that are free or cheap (a vital aspect for any student) and that take place close to your university.

Then spread the information about the events on the internet (Facebook is the obvious choice) and encourage people to attend. This will enhance your research, organisational and social skills and provide your fellow students with a chance to have fun, learn something useful, or both.

Invite interesting people to give talks

Every society is based around a particular point of interest. Sometimes, if a society is large, there are several points of interest.

One of the ways to benefit your fellow society members is to organise events, where you can invite people who can be considered an authority in your field of interest and ask them to talk about topics that would be of interest for the students. For example, a medical students' society could invite a nurse to talk about first aid – not only to the members of the society but also to anyone interested. An engineering society could invite a recruiter from a large engineering company or an experienced professional who can talk about working in the industry. A drama society can invite an actor or an actress to tell about his or her experience in the world of theatre. A business-oriented society can invite different entrepreneurs to give talks about business skills every week... Opportunities are endless! Your main task is to contact the person and get them to agree to come. Believe me, it's much easier than it sounds – people love talking about themselves and being listened to!

Promote the society inside and outside the university

Student societies would not survive without members. Therefore, you need to become an active promoter and marketer for your society.

Some societies find it easier to attract new members. For example, a person who wants to play football will look for a football club, inside or outside the university. However, a person who wants to improve their public speaking skills, learn French or get started in journalism might not even think that a student society or club can help him/her achieve these goals. If your society is not as high-profile as you would like it to be, you have to *make it* high-profile.

You have to start promoting it. This can be done in many ways – creating a Facebook page, a blog for your society where you showcase the interesting stuff you do, simple word-of-mouth marketing or even occupying a stand at Societies' Fair. There are numerous ways to do it, but internet-based marketing is the best and the most time and cost-efficient way (once again, I will tell you more about it in **Chapters 12 and 13**).

Active, effective marketing will increase the number of members and boost the society's budget through membership fees (one of the main sources of income for a society), which will allow you to plan more events. You will also get more 'pairs of working hands', which will make it easier and more interesting for you to do the work your society is meant to do.

56

So, it's all rather clear with promoting your society inside university – you do it to make people interested and to increase the number of members. But why do you need to promote it outside the university?

The reason is partially the same as above – to get people interested, especially since your future employers and (or) clients can be among those people. It's not as much about the society as about your work in it. You need to have a solid platform on which you can showcase your best work and create online proof that you have done certain things and done them well.

Some of you who are reading this might be the kinds of persons who do not like blowing their own trumpet. If you also think along those lines, it's time for a change. Being proud of your achievements is perfectly normal and talking about them is absolutely necessary in the modern, hectic world. Better learn it early on, while you still have time for learning more than your degree course demands – in your first and second years.

Put this all down on your CV

Once you have done all of this, you need to put all your positive results into a form that is acceptable to present to the people who will hire you (once again, as I have already said above, those are not necessarily your future managers; people who hire you can be your customers, your listeners, your readers – it all depends on what path you choose to take once you've graduated).

You need a CV, not only when you are applying for a corporate job. You need it all the time, for the information of your clients, readers, listeners, etc. It is vital to have information about your experience, as well as your professional and personal achievements available publicly (you must have an online copy of your CV on LinkedIn – I will talk more about it in **Chapter 12: Students and Online Presence**).

Next, I would like to share my experience of getting a work placement: how I gained employability skills and how it led me to my current professional path as an author-entrepreneur.

My Story:

How I Got a Work Placement in the Middle of the Recession

My placement experience was truly awesome: I spent a year working as a communications officer for The Science and Technology Facilities Council, a governmental research body. The nature of my work was mostly journalistic – researching, writing articles and reports, producing marketing materials and promotional videos. As far as I know, there is no such thing as a paid placement for a writer (unless you're extremely lucky), so this was as close as it could get and, in essence, I spent a year doing what I liked.

However, I am not writing this to say how great my experience was. I want to say how I landed this placement. Quite honestly, writing articles for a British research body is a challenging job. Back then, as an overseas student, I was fully aware of my (limited) language skills.

So, how does an overseas student get a job that may be more suited for a native speaker? Or, let's phrase it differently: how does a student of *International Relations and English* land a job in a *science* research council?

How to get a job without much relevant experience? For example, how does someone with a degree in humanities get a job in the banking sector? How does one convince the employer they are the best person for the job when there's a clear mismatch between their background and the nature of the job? Or, even more interestingly, how does one get a paid placement when the recession is menacing everyone?

During the course of my placement my boss told me a secret. You see, at least when it comes to placements (and, I believe, graduate training schemes as well) managers hire you not only because of what you are. They hire you because of what you have the potential to *become*.

My manager told me that they were looking not only for the best person to do the job. They were looking for someone whom they could teach the most. However, naturally, they saw this potential in me based on what I had already achieved. Therefore, in order for the managers to see what you can become you must present evidence that you *can* indeed become remarkable.

And this is the first and the most important secret of becoming employable: **you have to be willing to learn and show your ability to progress**. In other words, you've got to be open-minded. Forget words like 'you can't teach an old dog new tricks'. This does not apply to you – and if it does, you'd better change it. No matter what your degree background is, no matter what work experience you have, you've got to show them that you've learnt more from your 'irrelevant' experience than anyone who's worked in the field for several years has. Moreover, you have to be able to demonstrate that you are willing to learn the new job fast. The best way to do it is by providing other examples of learning fast.

Let me tell you about how I did it.

To begin with, I had wasted a lot of time. I had changed my course and I needed to think very hard what I could extract and 'transfer' from that year onto my CV. I lived a moderately-paced life filled with the usual activities like working, studying, socialising and occasionally enjoying solitude. Nothing special, nothing outstanding.

The largest part of the second year was spent in a similar fashion. The difference was that I loved my degree course. I thoroughly enjoyed what I was doing, indulging in my studies, reading books about linguistics and politics... yet, I stubbornly evaded taking direct action to develop my skills, except for the fact that I started writing more, making first steps in learning the craft. I got another job in the library as a writing mentor, where I taught students essay-writing skills. At the end of the year, when my contract with the library expired, I submitted the last assignment and went to London, where I got a job as a kitchen porter in a hotel.

It was there, when I was scrubbing the floor and washing plates that I realised: *uh-oh! I have to find a placement next year.*

It somehow came to me that I had a problem. Or maybe even several:

- The year of business studies was almost entirely wasted and it was all my fault. All I could bring to the table were my academic achievements, as well as limited customer service and spoken communication skills that I had developed in the retail job. It was far from enough.

- Gosh, I did not even know how to write a good CV! The only thing I knew was that my old one, which helped me get the retail job, was obsolete and it seemed to me that it had been written by a ten-year-old.

- The first year of International Relations and English was another example of time not-so-well spent. I could put my library job on my CV, but I still had to figure out how to turn my activities into achievements.

- Despite having a job where I taught people essay writing skills, my relationship with essays was sort of one-way. I knew how to correct a bad one, but I still didn't know the magic formula for a good one that would land me a First each time. There was a lot I had to learn about academic skills.

- I knew that I wanted to work in PR and communications (the closest field to creative writing and easier to get into than journalism), but had no idea how to start working towards that goal.

- (I'm really ashamed of this one) The average grade for the first year studying the subject I thoroughly enjoyed was lower than the one I got for the business studies. I had 65%: it was good, but it was still far from a First.

So, how did I get out of this situation and ended up a winner at the job interview?

Here are the lessons I have drawn for myself:

1. Start early and do your homework.

I did not wait for the start of the second year to begin researching job opportunities. The second year is one great 'Race against Time' – and I wanted to get well ahead of it. My job as a porter started at 7 am and finished at 3 pm. The rest of the day was free. So I signed up with the local library and invested time in summer education.

First of all, I picked up several books on CV writing, and, with their help, crafted the best CV I could from my meagre experience. I would add to it later, but now it was important to have the 'skeleton' and follow the main rules:

- Be precise. Forget vagueness and emphasise your achievements: skills gained, skills developed, number of people helped, lessons learnt, grades earned for essays, etc.
- Be proud. Make every tiniest achievement sound as if it is worth the Nobel Prize at least.
- Be bold. Use powerful language; more emphasis on action verbs.

(Unfortunately, I do not have much space in this book to talk about effective CV writing but you can find a lot of useful information in my free eBook called *How to Write a CV with Little or No Work Experience* that is available for free online, on *The Lecture Room* and *First Year Counts*).

Next, I read all I could find on public relations and effective written communication. I realised I had to do my homework in advance – because later, when the academic year started, I would have no time to do it unless I wanted to be sleep-deprived. After I was done with professional development, I decided to prepare for my studies as well. On my day off, I went back to my university, visited the library and took out several books that I knew would be on my reading list next year. This way, I managed to save a lot of time and, when autumn came and I became really busy, studying was easy at least because I already knew some lecture material.

Having spent the summer reading and preparing, I was ready to spring into real action in autumn.

2. Join a student society and start helping its executive committee. Then, since you are doing something anyway, co-ordinate a charity event.

Since I feel very strongly about protecting the planet and the rights of its inhabitants, I joined the Amnesty International/People and Planet society and started developing my skills in promotional work and communications.

I had had an idea to put together a conference on sustainability and green technologies for some time. In October, I started implementing this idea. It was an event that involved 10 presenters from three universities and lasted the entire afternoon. In the beginning, I did it all single-handedly. I emailed the people I wanted to invite. I scheduled the time that was suitable for all of them. I went to our events officer to ask her to help me book an empty lecture room and get some publicity. Then I realised I was not able to do it all by myself and did the only sensible thing – asked the events team and the marketing office for help.

I was lucky: they helped me with sorting out the catering (tea, coffee and biscuits), gave me some ideas about what else needed to be done (such as inviting the vice-chancellor and preparing name badges). Overall, the event was a success and even helped me win a university Student Guild award for outstanding services. All in all, it was just a piece of paper, but at that time it was a great ego booster!

One of the most important lessons that I've learnt through the experience was that all the lessons are learnt not after the action, but during it. The organisational process around that small conference taught me more about myself and about the world of work than any textbook or an entire semester of lectures would ever have.

I also started helping the society with its own events. We organised a protest against a certain bank that funded 'dirty energy' projects and I even got escorted out of the National Exhibition Centre by a grumpy security guard because of that – it was a lot of fun in retrospect, though. We baked cupcakes, sold them in a pub and sent the money we had raised to a rape crisis centre. I still remember that evening in a student flat, mixing the dough, getting things wrong, laughing, preparing the cakes and the icing, and then, the next day, selling them all in our university pub in the space of a couple of hours. Every time, I just loved the sense of community and the sense of achievement that never left me after I got involved.

I was never part of the executive committee. I never ran for elections. But it did not matter. Even today I think that being a positive, active member with no defined job title was a much better experience than being a passive Vice-President ever would have been. *When it comes to your CV, achievements matter much more than job titles*.

3. Look for every opportunity to develop your skills. Start locally. Find opportunities in what you are already doing.

I needed professional skills and more knowledge in the field of marketing and communications. Therefore, I needed to develop my written and spoken communication, public speaking and promotion skills. Here's how I did it:

First of all, I looked for a marketing gap among the activities I was already involved in. I worked from this presumption: hard work is good, but there is no need to take up ten thousand activities. *One job that is done well will make you proud. Ten that are done badly will make you tired*. The most obvious choice was my job in the library: we had recruited seven new people and all of us were idle half of the time because we lacked students who would like to get free friendly advice regarding their academic work. This was bad for two reasons (1) the employees had little chance to practise their skills and (2) we all wanted to get funding for the centre for the next year to continue working there, so we had to show we were active and efficient. Naturally, lack of students coming meant lack of any feedback we could receive on our work.

So, I took initiative and created a presentation about our services. Then I emailed the lecturers, asking them for a five-minute time slot in their lectures, during which I could talk to the students about the Learning Development Centre and invite them to use our free services.

The breakthrough happened after I went to a business studies lecture – I spoke in front of 400 people twice (there were 800 first year students in business-related courses that year). After that, all eight writing mentors forgot what idleness meant. We were fully booked until the end of the academic year.

Secondly, in order to develop my writing skills further, I became a journalist for the university newspaper. I could have put my academic essays as examples of my good writing skills on my CV, but academic writing and journalism are very different in style, and I thought it would benefit me to have experience in various fields. When I joined the newspaper, I immediately regretted not having done so before – but, after all, during my very first year I even did not realise that this possibility existed!

There is something about getting involved in university life not only socially but also professionally that makes it really worthwhile. When you are passive, you never hear of any opportunities that university offers. *However, once you become active at least in one area, you are spoilt for choice within two weeks*. I had to restrain myself from getting involved in too many things.

4. Start researching companies early.

If you're looking for a placement, start early – preferably in September. Why? Because come October-November everyone will start job-hunting and competition will be intense. You can bet that companies are more likely to pay attention to your application if it is one of the ten they receive in one day than if it is one of the fifty.

Pay close attention to all deadlines. Research what the company's requirements are and fill in the application form keeping to the requirements.

Thoroughly research each company you apply to. What does it do exactly? What are its aims? What is its mission statement? Its area of activity? Is it local or international? If international, in which countries are its offices based? Who are its main competitors? What are its strengths? How do your skills, education and work experience fit within the goals of the organisation?

You will need answers to these questions when writing a covering letter, filling out an application form or at the job interview when you will be asked what you know about the company or why you want to work there. You can find more information about researching those questions in **Chapter 9**, under the section 'Commercial Awareness'.

5. Fill your CV with achievements.

As soon as you get involved and become active, add details about your involvement onto your CV. Another important lesson I have learnt was that I did not even have to have completed my projects to list them as achievements. Work in progress looks just as good. So what if the events you are organising had have not taken place yet? It is work in progress, and it should receive a place of honour on your CV. After all, why not? It is your work, so be proud of it!

You can learn more about turning your usual student activities into achievements in **Chapter 10: Skills All Employers Require and Where to Get Them**.

In summary, I got the placement because I mustered all my physical and mental strength and, in a space of several months, did enough to impress the interviewers. I showed them that I was able to learn fast. I showed them that I had done my homework and was interested in the job and wanted to learn it well. I showed them that all my activities at university were in one way or another connected to the job I wanted to do. I showed that I was active and liked getting involved. However, I did not lose myself among my goals and still did what I enjoyed. I showed them that I could work to develop my skills, was able to work in a team and on my own, hold a job that pays the bills and work for free to help others. I demonstrated a can-do attitude and business-like approach to whatever project I undertook.

In other words, I was employable. Yet, as I said before, several years ago the world was different. In the modern world, I would also make use of the internet and social media to get my name out there and make people listen to my online voice because I've got something worthwhile to say. I will tell you all about it in **Chapters 12 and 13**. However, in the next chapter, I would like to talk more about transferable skills that students can learn at university and how you can use your daily student activities to your advantage. Let's get going!

CHAPTER 10

SKILLS ALL EMPLOYERS REQUIRE AND WHERE TO GET THEM

Several previous chapters have been dedicated to obtaining valuable skills. In this chapter, I will talk about those in more detail, giving you some tips on how to extract skills from almost everything you do at university, making every activity of yours a learning experience.

As I have already pointed out in the Introduction, the main problem that modern students face is not the lack of employment opportunities, but the lack of employability skills. Although modern graduates do have great degree-related skills, their weak point is the soft, or transferable, competencies.

I understand that some of you who are reading my book are not first year students anymore. I hope you spent your first year better than I did. However, even if you had been living a 'standard' student life until now, you still have a great chance to turn your 'usual' experiences into extraordinary achievements. For those who are in your first year, I hope that these tips will wake you up and put in your mind those burning questions: *What am I doing here? How do I make the most of my time and activities? How much can I learn from my experience? How much have I learnt from what I am doing now? What to do to learn more? Where can I learn more?*

Let's have a look at what skills employers ask for. Here's the standard list:

- Communication skills (written and spoken)
- Analytical and Research skills
- Teamwork skills
- Self-motivation
- Organisational abilities (especially time management)
- Commercial awareness
- Numeracy
- IT
- Foreign Languages
- Leadership

So, let's see how you can enhance those skills while at uni – and if you are closer to the end of your studies, what usual activities you can use as sources of those valuable skills.

Communication Skills (written and spoken)

One of the most obvious ways to enhance your communication skills at university is by writing assignments (essays, reports, research papers or your dissertation) and by giving presentations in front of the class. If your degree course involves these things (especially oral presentations, because that's the area in which many students do not have much experience), use every opportunity to practice your communication skills. Employers value employees who are able to express their thoughts clearly, in an organised manner.

Moreover, if your academic work is good, you could take it further and have it published in undergraduate research journals. After all, not many undergraduates can boast having publications and these achievements can add a competitive edge to your employability. I will tell more about undergraduate research opportunities in **Chapter 11**.

Other ways to enhance your written communication skills are blogging, writing for the university newspaper or volunteering as a writer for a website (especially useful for those who want to get into journalism and other professions where written skills are paramount).

When it comes to spoken communication, you can boost your skills by joining a debating society or a public speaking club. The latter is even better because you can speak on any topic, whilst debating societies are mostly politics-oriented. However, public speaking clubs are harder to find in universities. They are run by persons with a lot of experience in public speaking – teachers, maybe even actors – whose age range is well above that of an average student. Nevertheless, there's nothing stopping you from finding someone experienced in public speaking as well as a few people who wish to practice their skills, and establishing a little club of your own – I am pretty sure that such a person can be found and they will be willing to help you out. It only takes a little effort on your behalf!

Analytical and Research Skills

Once again, your academic work can help you here. Academic writing is all about looking for right information in the library and on the internet (research skills), selecting what is relevant to your assignment question, examining your findings and interpreting them, telling fact from opinion and being critical about your work and that of others, which means knowing the potential drawbacks of the dataset and the methods (analytical skills). You can find more information on assignment writing on *The Lecture Room* and *First Year Counts*.

By the way, humanities and social sciences students have a lot of potential to develop these skills because viewing a situation from all perspectives is basically what they do academically. In the humanities, unlike in exact sciences, it is normal that there can be several truths, rather than one that is 'absolute' and 'objective'.

Teamwork Skills

There are very few jobs in the modern world in which you will work on your own all the time. You will have to collaborate, to work with others, which means you need to show your teamwork skills.

Working in a team can mean many things: effective communication, being easy-going and open-minded, being a leader, taking initiative to complete tasks, dividing the tasks between the members so that everyone is motivated but not overloaded and everyone sharing a feeling that their contribution is meaningful.

University is a great place to develop your teamwork skills. Let's start with sports: each time you join a sports club, you join a team. Even if it is a sport like karate or fencing, where you fight alone against your opponent, when you take part in a competition, you are part of your university's team. In sports like football or basketball, it is even more obvious: the outcome depends on collective effort and an effective mechanism of working together is paramount.

Another way to enhance your teamwork skills is being a member of a non-sport society and helping the executive committee (see the previous chapter). Once you take initiative, you become part of their team – and now it's up to you to pull your weight. If you do it well, you can achieve quite a lot, and then proudly put it down on your CV.

University assignments will help you here as well – but only if they are group assignments. When working on a group project, you will inevitably have to divide the tasks, assume responsibilities, and, if the group is not doing too well, someone will have to take initiative and make sure the team starts functioning more effectively.

Another great way to develop your teamwork as well as organisational skills is to establish a study group for exam revision. It works according to the same principle: the tasks are divided between the members, everyone is pulling their weight, team meetings are organised, and everyone is responsible and willing to help one another. Give it a try – it will take some effort in the beginning to make the gears spin, but it's totally worth it.

Self-motivation

One of the larger issues that the world of work has with the academic world is too much emphasis on individual tasks and too little attention to group assignments – especially in arts, humanities and social sciences. Of course, this is a problem, but another skill you can develop thanks to this feature of higher education is taking initiative and working independently.

Despite what I said above – that organisations emphasise teamwork – in real life you can often be left on your own to deal with a task. Moreover, employers value workers who do not need a manager breathing down their neck to do the job and feel motivated.

Apart from your academic work, you could also take initiative and co-ordinate an event, like I did with the conference on sustainability (see **Chapter 8**). In paid work experience and volunteering, the best jobs to develop these are street fundraising and cold calling. Still, I believe that nothing motivates you to work on your own initiative as much as a project you undertake because you want to, not because you have to. Just take initiative and do something for pleasure! It can be absolutely anything – organise a concert, found an undergraduate research journal or establish a knitting and crocheting club. It's not the title of the project that matters, but your determination to start it, your strength to see it through and your persistence to finish it successfully.

Organisational skills

Once you get into university, developing a realistic schedule is paramount. First of all, unlike in school or college, your study hours are irregular. You can have two days full, two days free and then a seminar on Friday afternoon that splits your entire day in a most inconvenient manner. With few contact hours and a lot of time for independent study, you can feel like you have very little to do – and maybe even be tempted to make other plans and skip some classes. However, I advise you to take advantage of the study hours and skip as little as possible – not least because you're paying for your lectures. Plus, it is obvious that it will be much easier to do well in your exams if you attend classes. Secondly, you can easily get confused if you have too many activities: your lectures, seminars, labs, society meetings, attempts to find a part-time job, lack of time when you find one, etc. Finally, it is absolutely vital that you use your free time wisely, doing things when they need to be done and using the time when you are most awake and energetic to accomplish the most difficult tasks.

As I said above, the first year is an introduction to university life – both its academic and the social side. It allows you to understand how this system works, find your unique academic writing style, meet a lot of intelligent people, realise where you stand as a person and as a future professional, what you like, what you're good at, and so on. Becoming organised in your first year means that you won't have to do it later, when the time comes to look for a placement and take your studies more seriously. So get yourself a diary and regard every free minute as a chance to do something useful. Re-read your lecture notes right after the lectures to retain the material better. Study in that two-hour break between the classes. If you're an early riser (and you should become one if you're not), some research before the morning lectures will also benefit you, be it for your studies or your work. Since you will also (I hope) be actively involved in the life of a student society or two, try to get minor society-related things sorted out in those short breaks – you can bet they will seem *short*. Try to fill all your time with useful activities – whatever you define as useful.

Commercial awareness

It's a bit strange that someone who quit a course in business studies to study a subject that he likes speaks about commercial awareness. Yet, when I changed my course, I knew what I was doing. I had a vision of how to make a living out of what I liked and already had mapped out a success strategy (a bit schematic in the beginning but as time passed, it fleshed out and became a working plan).

Whatever degree you're doing, you must never adopt the 'boycott all things corporate' attitude. As I have already said above, when I say 'people who hire you' I also mean 'people who will want to sponsor your art'. When I say 'employability', I mean skills for life, not just for the job.

Moreover, for most jobs, even corporate ones, a business degree is not required. What is required, however, is interest in the organisation and thinking about it from a business perspective – ways it can make (or raise) money, ways it can attract customers/visitors/fans, how it can market itself to make itself known to the wider public or persuade people to use its products or services, who its main competitors are, etc.

So, how do you develop your commercial awareness? First, select the field whose business-like aspects you would like to investigate. It can be the actual business market, or the field of higher education, environmental issues, the IT sector, the public sector, science and technology, medicine, writing and publishing... The choice is yours – every sector of human activity, profit or non-profit, does have a business perspective. Next, enrich your knowledge of the field and keep up-to-date by reading relevant press, listening to the radio, looking for the news in your chosen area, watching current affairs programmes, etc.

After that, get some work experience: start doing something either in a part-time job or by becoming active in a student society, and observe yourself and others. Try to answer the following questions:

What is your preferred working style? How does the team function? Which members manage the team? Who works with their head down and who is in the spotlight? How do you prefer to work? What motivates you? What challenges you?

Numeracy

It is true about many jobs that they take people with any degree: a sociology graduate can become an accountant; an English graduate can find a job in human resources or even an investment bank. Many doors are open. However, in order to obtain a job in a business-related field, you have to know some maths.

Many people, especially in arts, humanities and social sciences, like to say they are not good at maths. Actually, I am not too good either. However, I am very grateful to my maths teacher for telling me a secret that helped me get through the final exams at school, maths-based modules at university and numerical reasoning tests during job applications.

The secret is very simple: being good at maths is not about knowledge at all; it is all about practice.

Moreover, I have some great news for those who dread the word 'numerical': when it comes to numeracy skills needed at work, you do not have to calculate the area of a complex multi-angular shape or perform sophisticated statistical tests. All you have to do is to learn how to add, subtract, multiply and divide quickly and efficiently. It's also beneficial to learn how to read graphs and extract information from tables. If you feel you need that, it can be learnt by practising a little bit every day.

As with almost everything, university is the best place to improve your maths skills. I am pretty sure that your university has a math drop-in centre where people who are really good with figures can help you if you seek it. Books on preparation for numerical tests are also available from your university library.

Information Technology (IT)

The definition of *sound IT skills* can vary from person to person. For some it's merely the ability to format a Word document and to create an acceptable spreadsheet; for others, it means being able to write a working piece of software in a matter of hours. My understanding of this concept is closer to the first definition. Having sound IT skills means being able to work with most popular Office applications (Word, Excel and PowerPoint), conduct efficient internet-based research and have a good sense of email etiquette.

You can learn all of this during your studies. Once again, your academic assignments can be extremely helpful. However, they cannot be the only source because if they are, there will be a lot of trial-and-error learning. What I really want you to do is to go to the library, borrow some books that teach you to work with basic Office applications and read them thoroughly (ideally while you still are in your first year). This will teach you a few useful things – for example, how to select a part of a text without using your mouse or touchpad, or how to jump straight to line 19 on page 61 of the 200-page document without doing all that scrolling. This might not seem much to you now, but believe me – knowing these little things will save you a lot of time in the future.

Foreign languages

This one is a matter of great debate: on the one hand, every official from every education department says that Britain should invest more into foreign language learning and teaching as the country loses millions of pounds through lost business opportunities because the seller and the buyer do not speak the same language; on the other hand, it is true that languages are difficult to learn and not everyone has the time, the aptitude, or the willingness to do it.

However, in this book I am not talking about what you want. I am talking about what the people who will hire you want and how you can obtain it. University is a great place to learn and practice foreign languages for several reasons. First of all, it is the best place to meet educated people from different countries. You can brush up on your French, German, Spanish or Italian that might have got a bit rusty since the GCSEs, or even learn a new language. If you find enough enthusiasts, you can even establish a language learning group; joining a language-based society is also a great option. Secondly, there are plenty of websites where podcasts and lesson guides for language learning are offered for free. The beauty of podcasts is that you can load them onto your MP3 player and listen to them almost any time you want – while cleaning, cooking, commuting, or preparing to go to bed. Finally, although it may not always seem so, university offers you a lot of free time – much more than a full-time job would, not to mention managing your own business. Therefore, using this time to learn a new skill is the best you can do!

Leadership

First of all, let's define what a leader is. To me, a leader is a person who can spot a problem before anyone else does and solve it – whether by himself/herself or with the help of other people. Leaders must have most of the skills I have mentioned in this chapter. They must be able to communicate effectively, to work hard on their own and in a team, be good planners and able to analyse situations from all angles. Moreover, they must have great interpersonal skills, be friendly and helpful.

Some people think that leadership is something they can never achieve. 'I'm a follower, not a leader,' they say. My response to this is the following: there are too many people who are using these words as an excuse for their reluctance to become great at what they're doing. There is no need for more.

Get involved, develop the skills I listed above and you will be a leader – I can assure you of that. All it takes is just a little courage and practice.

In short, if you are just starting your studies, then prepare to double your speed and develop these skills. However, if you are nearing the end of your course, then reflect upon everything you have done at university and start extracting little achievements. Everything you do at university can help: that study group you started in order to revise for the toughest exams, that great game of football you played when your university team finally broke into the semi-finals and that top-class essay you wrote in your second year. Anything and everything can be a source of successfully learning the skills needed in the real world.

CHAPTER 11

A FEW WORDS ON UNDERGRADUATE RESEARCH

As I already pointed out in the previous chapter, your academic assignments can be a great source of transferable employability skills. Your essays (either with a given topic or the topic of your choice), exams and dissertations can teach you a lot about written communication, organisational and time management skills, teamwork, self-motivation, IT skills, technicalities of research and analysis, etc. However, you can take your academic work even further: you can use your assignments to make yourself more employable.

There are two main ways to do this. The first one is merely to include your assignments in your CV (if your marks are high, I advise you to do this in any case, especially if the topics of those assignments are relevant to the job you are applying for). The second way is by getting your academic work published.

11.1. Academic achievements and your CV

Let's talk first about putting your academic achievements on your CV. There are two main reasons why you should do that:

1. Your academic work is the testimony of your professional abilities

The people who hire you don't know you. They don't know what you are like. However, your academic achievements (not just an average grade for the year, but specific grades for each subject) can tell them quite a lot. First of all, if you've made effort for your degree, it is more likely that you will also make effort for your job. If you have shown examples of hard work, resilience, research skills and analytic insight for an essay, you will also show it for a quarterly report you will have to do – even if the subject you've studied is not very relevant to the job.

2. If your degree is relevant to the job you're applying for, your assignments can make a huge difference

Imagine an engineering graduate the title of whose dissertation was *'The influence of the use of bio-fuels on internal combustion engine efficiency'*. Imagine how helpful this would be when applying for a job in the bio-fuels industry! Or an English graduate trying to get into journalism who has written two essays with a free topic, as well as his dissertation, on various aspects of the language of the news media. Coupled with some experience – even if it is writing for his own blog and the university newspaper – this boosts his chances of success enormously. A biology graduate who wants to do a Master's in medicine and has written her dissertation on chemical reactions to certain types of drugs in the body is much more likely to get onto that Master's programme than she would had she decided to write her final year project on ecosystems.

In short, if you feel that a certain assignment of yours is relevant to the job you want to do, do not hesitate to put it on your CV. It shows that you like the subject, that you're genuinely interested in the area and that you want to learn more about it – all of which raises your profile in the employers' eyes, and this is what we are aiming for.

11.2. Publishing your academic work

Publishing your academic work is a great way to get ahead of the crowd of graduates – after all, not many students can boast having publications. The best way to publish your work is by submitting it to an undergraduate research journal. In order to be published, it has to fulfil two conditions: it must be your original research (otherwise known as a 'free topic' essay) and it must have received a high grade. If you want, of course, you can submit something marked below 60%, but then expect to see 'substantial revisions' on the comment sheet, and you'd better know how to revise an academic paper.

Undergraduate research is not as big in the UK as it is in the USA, but it's catching up pretty fast. There are quite a few undergraduate research journals in the UK and, since the year 2010, the British Council for Undergraduate Research (BCUR) has been hosting undergraduate research conferences where aspiring researchers present their work.

Here are some useful links for you if you consider submitting your work for publication:

Journals:

Title: *Reinvention*
University: Warwick
Subject: All accepted
URL: http://www2.warwick.ac.uk/fac/cross_fac/iatl/ejournal/

Title: *Diffusion: the UCLan Journal of Undergraduate Research*
University: University of Central Lancashire
Subject: All accepted, but you have to be a student at UCLAN
URL: http://www.uclan.ac.uk/diffusion

Title: *Début: The Undergraduate Journal of Languages, Linguistics and Area Studies*
University: Southampton
Subject: Languages, linguistics, area studies
URL:
http://www.studyinglanguages.ac.uk/student_voices/debut

Title: *Pixel: The Cambridge Undergraduate Journal of Development Economics*
University: Cambridge
Subject: Economic development
URL: http://www.pixelthejournal.com

Title: *Ideate: the Undergraduate Journal of Sociology*
University: Essex
Subject: Sociology
URL:
http://www.essex.ac.uk/sociology/research/publications/stu
dent_journals/ug/default.aspx

Title: *The British Journal of Undergraduate Philosophy*
University: Oxford
Subject: Philosophy
URL: http://www.bups.org/bjup-online/

Title: *The Plymouth Student Scientist*
University: Plymouth
Subject: Science and Technology. Not sure if you have to be a student in Plymouth, but I think you do.
URL:
http://www.theplymouthstudentscientist.org.uk/index.php/ps
s

Title: *Geoversity*
University: Oxford Brookes
Subject: Geography; one has to be a student at Oxford Brookes.
URL: http://www.brookes.ac.uk/schools/social/geoversity

Title: *Earth and E-nvironment*
University: Leeds
Subject: Environmental science; one has to be a student in the University of Leeds.

URL:
http://homepages.see.leeds.ac.uk/~lecmsr/ejournal/index.ht
m

Title: *BURN*
University: Nottingham
Subject: Biosciences
URL: http://www.nottingham.ac.uk/~sbzml/

Title: *Bioscience Horizons*
University: Oxford
Subject: Biosciences
URL: http://biohorizons.oxfordjournals.org/

Title: *Enquiry: The ACES Journal of Undergraduate Research*
University: Sheffield Hallam
Subject: Arts, Computing, Engineering and Sciences. One has to be a student in Sheffield Hallam to contribute.
URL:
http://research.shu.ac.uk/aces/enquiry/index.php/enquiry/in
dex

The problem with those journals is that more often than not they are connected to one particular university and it is hard to get published in them if you study elsewhere. However, the U.S. has a large number of well-established journals and the Council of Undergraduate Research in the U.S. lists many of them on their page:

http://www.cur.org/resources/students/undergraduate_j
ournals/

Hope this helps. Enjoy your academic research and best of luck!

CHAPTER 12

STUDENTS AND ONLINE PRESENCE (BE SEEN)

The next two chapters will be dedicated to the fourth and the fifth steps on the path towards success: becoming well-known on the internet for being unselfish and helpful. However, before we move on to that, I would like to talk about the potential pitfalls of student online presence.

Online professionalism is increasingly important in the modern world. This includes presenting yourself on the internet in the best possible light and making your name known for sharing quality information with others. This will be the subject of this chapter, as well as the next one.

12.1. Why Does a Modern Student Need Online Presence?

Seriously, why? And don't we all have it already? When I was a Fresher, the most common question people were asking during the Freshers' Week was 'Are you on Facebook?' Nowadays, the entire world is on Facebook or Twitter, or both. Universities, their lecturers, their careers services, every student, their dog and the dog's uncle are online! What need for online presence am I talking about?

It is true – social media have hijacked our lives. I am sure that some psychotherapists somewhere in the United States are cashing in, treating people for Facebook addiction. But when it comes to what this book is all about, having a Facebook account is **not** an online presence. Nor is being on Twitter, Flickr, Tumblr, Digg, LinkedIn, StumbleUpon, Pinterest or anywhere else.

Why does it **not** count as online presence?

The answer is simple: **because it's not useful for you**. Moreover, certain elements of an online presence can be quite harmful to a modern, carefree student.

So, let's discuss why you need a strong – and, above all, professional – online presence. There are several reasons:

1. Employers recruit via social media.

Recruiting an employee is an expensive, resource-intensive process, and employers do whatever works for them and whatever saves money. At the moment, social media are doing a really good job. According to the latest surveys carried out by a U.S.-based job platform Jobvite, 92% of employers use social networks and social media to recruit people. Two thirds of companies use Facebook, 54% rely on Twitter. LinkedIn (about which I will talk in section 12.2) is used by an amazing 93%. If employers go online, so should job seekers. The American trend will come to the UK in no time. Moreover, job seekers should behave professionally and respectfully since employers are watching them.

2. People 'google' people.

Yes, this one blows, but it's life. Your future employers are more and more likely to search you up on the internet. In fact, the Jobvite survey has found that three out of four recruiters said they do check a candidate's online profile, with 48% doing it all the time. Typing a person's name into a search bar is one of the fastest ways to get the first impression about them and to find out whether they are lying about themselves on their CV, or not. Moreover, it can expose some things you would not want your employer to know – employers cringe not only at references to drugs, alcohol and foul language, but also at spelling and grammar mistakes, Jobvite survey claims.

Therefore, make sure your Facebook and Twitter accounts look presentable (I will talk about this in more detail later).

3. The Internet is a public place.

With all the buzzing and bubbling social media, the internet no longer offers you privacy or anonymity. Your words can become public very easily, even though you post them on a 'private' Facebook wall or Twitter page – so you've got to mind your language and really weigh your words carefully.

So, let's discuss *professionalism* online. Before I start talking about what you need to do, let's talk about what you're already doing. I am sure you have a Facebook account. Being on Facebook is a great opportunity to network and meet interesting people. However, in order for it to work best for you, your Facebook page has to show you in the best light.

A standard student Facebook account (a case of typical 'online presence') contains the following elements:

- Statuses like 'OMG our new lecturer is so cute!' or 'Bah! Soooo much homework and it's only the second week!'
- Photos from the last week's parties
- Photos from a cheap holiday in Spain taken during the Reading Week
- Complaints about how fast the loan money is running out
- Status updates related to other 'important' bits of your life like hangover, boyfriends/girlfriends, essay word counts and what's happening outside your window
- Quiz results: 'Which Prince Are You?'; 'Which Vegetable Reflects Your Personality?', etc.

There is nothing bad *per se* with having some of these elements on your Facebook wall. However, you really want to put yourself in the employer's shoes and go through your entire account with a fine-tooth comb. If you have any of the following, I want you to remove them as soon as possible:

- Any photos in which you are holding a drink in your hand (unless it is *obviously* a soft drink; a mug of tea is also fine)
- Any photos in which you are surrounded by dubious people. It could be a random party where you went by chance; however, if you are pictured in a neutral way, but two other people in the photo are downing vodka straight from the bottle, it may not be a good idea for this photo to be associated with your Facebook profile. Untag or, if possible, delete those pictures
- Any postings on your wall – photos, links, status updates, etc. – that might be considered offensive; the way to determine it is very easy: if you think it might be offensive, it probably is
- Any posting on your wall – photos, links, status updates, etc. – that make a reference to drugs, alcohol, sex, foul language, violence, racism, sexism or someone's level of intelligence
- Any comments or wall posts left by other people on your wall that might be considered offensive. The reasoning for this is the following: if someone makes a derogatory comment to you in real life, you might challenge them on it. If you do not, it means that you agree with that comment, right? So you'd better remove anything potentially harmful from your wall and challenge that person – face to face or in writing.
- Anything that could be considered too personal or too unprofessional for a workplace

All these elements are desirable in order for your Facebook page to be presentable. Funny pictures and tasteful anecdotes are also acceptable on social media pages, but something else is necessary as well, and that is evidence of what you have done to build a **community**.

Nowadays your community in both the *workplace* and the *world* is more important than it has ever been before. Your community forms the foundations of your future career, whatever path you choose. As I said, your community means the people you know, the people who know you, who consider you trustworthy and authoritative in certain matters. In other words, the people who will listen to you.

So, what does it mean to have a *Community*?

- It can mean having 2000 friends on Facebook, 200 of whom regularly like and comment upon your status updates (however, do not go for the numbers only – go for loyalty!)
- It means having more people follow you on Twitter than you are following
- It means having a blog with regular readers and lots of comments. Your blog can have 'curious visitors' but that is not enough. You need *fans*

Building a community of fans is vital in the modern world, and the best way to do it is to have a blog. I will cover blogging in the next chapter. For now, let's get some other things straight with the social media.

What I have said about Facebook above also applies to Twitter and other social media that are more personal than professional. However, there is also an online network that I would like you to pay special attention to. It's called LinkedIn.

12.2. A Few Words about LinkedIn

LinkedIn is known as a social network for connecting older professionals. In fact, the average age of a typical LinkedIn user is 45 years. This might put students off it and make them think that LinkedIn is not for them. If you also believe this, think again.

First of all, you do not even have to have a job to join LinkedIn. Students can benefit from it no less than experienced professionals can, and the sooner you start using it, the better – after all, if you do it now, you will not have to do it later.

If you start using it now, by the time you graduate you will have built a comprehensive profile where you will be able to list everything you have achieved during your studies, as well as all your work experience in student jobs, internships, volunteering and involvement in student societies. The networking site even has a student portal which recommends jobs based on your education and interests.

So, let's see what you can do using LinkedIn. Here are several ideas:

1. Showcase your studies and academic achievements;

2. Showcase your volunteer work and society involvement. As soon as you get involved, you can write about it on LinkedIn;

3. If you already have a part-time job but don't want to add your boss on Facebook, LinkedIn is your network. You can add your boss and your lecturers;

4. Get recommendations from your lecturers and employers at your student jobs. You can also get recommendations from members of student societies and your classmates – provided they are also on LinkedIn;

5. Join groups related to your studies and interests;

6. Keep updating your profile each time something new happens; whenever you get a new job, join a new society or take initiative to organise a project, add it to your LinkedIn profile;

7. Invite your lecturers and classmates to connect on LinkedIn;

8. Add the URL of your LinkedIn profile to your CV;

9. Include a professional photograph (e.g. in a formal suit).

In short, join LinkedIn as soon as possible and start benefiting from it. Do not regard it as a network for older professionals – join confidently because you are also a professional – albeit a young one – and live up to that proud title!

12.3. Modern Students and Blogging

Why is having a blog so important?

Because a blog is an online place where you present your abilities and have a constant, solid proof that you exist. It's funny, but it is the case – in the modern world, you must have your name online. Ideally, on a site that belongs to you. You must be easy to find. This way, people will know that you exist, that you do some serious work and have good results to show for it.

In other words, you have to stop waiting to be selected from 1000 other candidates with a degree in X. You have to start behaving proactively and reaching out to people. You need to make meaningful connections – and by this I mean not only knowing influential producers who will put you in front of a loving audience. *I mean knowing the audience itself.* In this book, I call it *'belonging to a Community'*. Naturally, this does not come on its own. A community is something you earn.

So, how do you do it?

Building a great, strong online presence is hard. The Internet is like a roaring crowd – a lot of noise and no visibility. This is why those who try to shout loudly, promoting themselves, often remain anonymous. They might be great, but the audience just does not hear them. It's like busking in the street. You might be lucky and have a top Broadway producer walk past you at the right time, but you might also end up with no more than a handful of coins in your hat – if someone decides to drop some in, that is.

So, how do you get heard?

Just like in a roaring crowd of graduates (see **Chapter 7**), the only way to get heard is to lean towards the person that is standing close to you and say something in their ear. Once they are interested, you can start talking. That person can also reach someone else's ear and this way, your words will spread. It will be slower than shouting what you want to say into the microphone from the stage, but, in your situation there is no way to get to the microphone anyway.

So, start making individual conversations.

Now, how is that one done?

Jeff Goins (www.goinswriter.com), a great, motivating writer and blogger and one of the people who inspired me to write this book, says that every person who wants to be heard in the noisy Internet crowd needs three things:

- A platform
- A brand
- Channels of communication

I shall borrow those terms from him and adapt them to my student audience.

Your platform is the place on the internet where you publish anything that is related to you as a professional. Your brand is the name or the sign people recognise you by. Your channels of communication and social media are the means of making links to your blog.

This is vital:

Your Facebook, Twitter, LinkedIn and other social media accounts should serve as channels of communication that lead people to your blog. Having a blog is a must for every modern student – because your blog is the place where you can speak to people and make individual conversations that lead to professional connections.

CHAPTER 13

A SHORT BLOGGING COURSE

As I said in the previous chapter, the best way to become known for being helpful is having a blog. However, in order for your blog to be successful, you must follow certain rules. The most obvious ones are the following: it must be relevant, useful to your readers, visually pleasing and interactive. Luckily, even if you are new to blogging, it is extremely easy to set one up. Websites that host blogging platforms are very user-friendly. However, before you start blogging about whatever comes to your mind, you need to consider the following elements:

13.1 Personal or Professional?

Is your blog personal or professional? The difference between the two is pretty straightforward: a personal blog is about you, and a professional blog is about others. The purpose of a personal blog is to introduce your reader to your rich inner world, make them interested in your life and/or your creative side. This can be your diary, poetry, thoughts and opinions on current affairs and your philosophy of life. Nothing wrong with that, but it is usually most effective if you are well-known already.

The purpose of a professional blog is to help people by giving them information they need on a certain subject.

When it comes to developing your employability skills, professional blogging is, of course, your first choice. When running a professional blog, you develop a particular set of skills:

- Research and analytical skills by researching information for your articles and selecting what is relevant
- Written communication skills by producing crisp, clear articles full of great advice and helpful information
- IT skills by playing around with the blogging software and formatting the text and the images so that they would look great on the Web (once again, do not worry about it too much because blogging platforms are very intuitive and easy to use. Moreover, at the initial stages you will not have to learn programming or HTML; you will only have to do this if you want to take your blogging further)

Of course, when it comes to blogging, there is no black or white. Adding a dash of personal to your professional blog (for example, an opinion article or a personal story) will only do you good and make you appear like a normal human being, not just like a quality content-generating machine. The only rule is to make it relevant to the blog's topic – which is the second aspect you need to consider.

13.2. The Topic

What is your blog about? Is it about medicine? Politics? Opening your own business? Cooking student budget meals? Academic writing? Getting a job in chemical engineering?

Do not think big. Think small and narrow – this is how the topic of your blog should be. You cannot write about everything – so do not try to please the entire world. Please a small part of it, and do it well.

The number of topics is enormous. What makes it more complicated is deciding on whose behalf you are writing. For example, I write for two blogs – *The Lecture Room* where I post advice for students on behalf of the founders of that blog (that's connected to my old platform *First Year Counts* where you can find my books and some free resources for students), and

Eynhallow Books, where I write my fiction and post advice for aspiring writers.

In your case, you manage the blog either on your own, or on behalf of a student society to which you belong (by the way, as I said above, even if the blog is about the society, you can have some personal posts there as long as they are related to the blog's topic). If you are running a blog as a member of a society, not only will you share useful information related to the society's area of activity, but also will write about what the society does, showcase its achievements, publish photos from events, etc.

There is only one rule you've got to follow when deciding on the topic: it must be interesting to you. You will have to research the topic, you will write about it all the time – so choose something that you feel passionately about. There is no need to write a blog if the process makes you suffer.

Once you decide on the topic, stick to it. Of course, there are many aspects of the same topic – for example, if your blog is about engineering, you can also write an article about a forward-looking theatre group that uses superb machinery for its production of *Macbeth*, and describe how that machinery works, making the show truly spectacular. All of your posts must be related to the main theme in one way or another – but there's a lot of flexibility as well.

The reason why your blog must be focused is also related to the third aspect you need to consider.

13.3. The Audience

Who will read your blog?

This is a very important question because you can't be all things to everyone. If you target everyone, you will reach no one.

When defining your audience, you cannot think of a group of people. You must think of one person who will benefit the most from your blog. What kind of person is it? *Whom* do you want to help (or to entertain)? The answer to this question will determine the content for the majority of your blog posts.

Most probably you will write for students – young people of your age in higher (maybe also further) education. But what are the students in your audience interested in? Are they interested in curious news and articles related to their area of study? Or are they interested in getting a job in a particular field? Maybe they are interested in revision techniques and something that would help them combat exam-related stress? Each of those groups of people want different things and what they want will determine your topics as well as the way you write about them.

Moreover, do not forget that students' needs can be seasonal – even when it comes to one area like academic success, essays and dissertations can be of greater interest in autumn and early spring because there is a lot more time to write them, and exam tips are more important during the winter and spring holidays when everyone is revising or at least pretending to do so. As summer approaches, a blogger who writes about academic success might want to write an article about incorporating good grades, as well as skills that academic assignments can teach one, into a CV because their audience will be looking for vacation work, etc.

As you can see, details like these are vital for a blogger. *Always write with your audience in mind*. After you've decided on the first three points, you should consider the three elements I have mentioned in the previous chapter: the platform, the brand and the channels of communication.

13.4. The Platform

This one is simple: the platform is the online location for your blog. This is where you post your articles, photos, podcasts or whatever you want to post. One of the greatest advantages of blogging (especially important for students) is that it is free. There are many platforms to choose from, but the most popular ones are Blogger.com, Wordpress.org and Tumblr.com. You can set up a free account on any of them and start developing your blog-website right away. They are all user-friendly, but the best one to my view is Wordpress – it's the one I use. They also have a great discussion forum if you have any technical questions, so for someone starting out, Wordpress is the perfect choice.

13.5 The Brand

The brand is what you are recognised by. It is a word or a symbol that is recognised immediately, even when seen or heard only partially. Words like Pepsi, Mercedes, NHS, Waterstone's or Harvard are immediately recognised and associated with certain qualities of a product or a service. You should also become a brand known at least in narrow circles.

Your brand can be your name, your nickname or the name of a student society that you represent. Your logo can also be anything – even your photo. It does not have to be professionally designed. However, if you feel it should be, there's nothing stopping you.

It is important to be recognisable by being consistent: use the same images for the blog, the Facebook page and the Twitter account.

One last thing you want to consider when creating a brand is choosing it wisely because it will be the name and the logo you will be recognised by in the future – so think about the best way of designing it, create it and start blogging!

13.6. The Channels of Communication

The best way to make your blog popular is to do some direct marketing. Share links to it on social media. It does not even take that long – set aside half an hour for the job each time you want to share a post. Moreover, many blogging platforms have special 'share' buttons wired to social media sites. For example, in Wordpress, you can share your blog post with multiple groups on LinkedIn, Facebook, Twitter, Digg,

StumbleUpon and many other social networks. Here's how you can do it more efficiently:

- Find groups and pages on Facebook that are related to the topic of your blog; join the groups and 'Like' the pages.
- Find similar groups on LinkedIn and join them, too.
- Find people on Twitter whose interests are based around the topic of your blog.
- Create a Facebook page about your blog; invite people to like it.
- Regularly update your blog and post useful, helpful links on social media. To make posting on Facebook more efficient, create a Word document with links to all the Facebook groups and pages related to the topic of your blog and open all the links from there. This way you will not have to search those groups and pages each time you want to post.
- In order not to have to manage multiple social media accounts, connect your Facebook to Twitter (there are many how-to articles online that explain how to do it). Facebook is easy to manage and you use it much more often anyway!
- Follow the 80/20 rule of generosity: 80% of your posts should be about others (other blogs, interesting articles, pictures relating to the topic of your blog, etc.) and 20% – about yourself, your own blog. Promote yourself, but also promote others. Eventually, others will notice it and start promoting you in response.
- Post helpful information and useful tips, but do not forget about the lighter content – there's always space for humour and fun, so funny pictures or jokes are not out of place on your social media accounts.

And now, let's move to the most important section of this chapter:

13.7. What You Can Do through Your Blog, or *the Power of Unselfishness*

This section is about being unselfish. It is about things you can do through a blog in order to help people – for free, of course – and become famous for being helpful.

First of all, let's consider why helping people for free is good for you. There are quite a few reasons.

- **People do not expect it.** In the words of Jeff Goins, we live in the world of 'me first' and 'gimme gimme'. When someone does something good for free, it takes people by surprise – and the element of surprise is an extremely powerful thing.

- **People love free stuff.** Especially if that stuff benefits them in some way. The first thing you have to do when you establish your blog is to create a product of value and quality, and give it away for FREE. For example, I have a free eBook on CV writing on *The Lecture Room* and many free resources for essay writing on *First Year Counts*, not to mention all the content on both sites for which you don't need to pay a single penny, either. Your product does not have to be an eBook – it can be anything that your readers will find useful.

- **It is fun.** It may sound unusual at first, but being generous is a very enjoyable experience. When you start blogging about something that others find useful and helpful, and also get positive feedback for your work, it makes you want to do more of this.

There are quite a few ways to be helpful via your blog. Here are some ideas:

- Create an eBook and make it free via your blog. The eBook must be of good quality and its topic has to be something people care about. ***How-to* and *self-help*** are the surest options. The best way to give people access to it is by creating an 'enter your name and email' form via a newsletter generation site, such as Mailchimp.com, and it's free to set up an account, just like it is to set up a blog.

- Write posts about something interesting or useful. For example, your blog can contain your lecture notes – then you can spread the word among the people from your course and get a grateful audience. Students from other universities who are also doing a similar course will be interested as well. Please, do not fear that now once you've put the lecture notes out on the Web, everyone will use your ideas in the exam. Only those who care will use the notes – there will be many who will try to learn them in the last night before the exam, and we all know how 'efficient' that usually is. In addition, you are not in competition with anyone, remember? It is you who is creating the blog, not others; it is your initiative and your ideas – and employers value the creator much more than the consumer.

- Set aside a special time slot for collecting interesting news related to the topic of your blog and post them in a bunch like a small 'news digest'. You can do it on a weekly basis so that not too much time is spent on this.

- If you are blogging about your society, write about the most interesting things you guys do. Anything goes here – events, socials, your usual activities... It's also a good idea to post to-do lists and decisions taken in society meetings.

13.8. Final Remarks

Blogging can be a lot of fun. It takes some effort to create posts, but, at least in my view, it feels great to see the results of your work – especially if people are reading what you write, find it useful, like it, share it, and comment upon it.

So, choose a subject you like, think what you know about it and share your knowledge. Inform, teach, or entertain someone – your hard work will pay off!

CONCLUSION

ATTEN-TION!

(The game of paintball is not over yet, remember?)

So, I've said all I wanted to say in this book. I have shared my personal advice on making the most out of your time at university. I have taught you how you can take advantage of the fact that you are at university to gain valuable work experience, to get involved in some purposeful activities, to enhance your profile and acquire skills – not only for work, but also for life.

You still have a few years of safe-play ahead of you. Whatever happens in that time, you've still got your university to provide you with education, a social status and multiple chances to succeed. However, once you return your graduate cap and gown where you took them from on your graduation day, the paintball match will be over. The real war will start, but if you are prepared, there will be no need to panic.

I have told you how to survive the great struggle called university and be prepared to win the war. I have taught you what I could. The rest is up to you. Go out there and apply those skills.

Make a plan right now!

Get a diary and start planning your time. Note all the busy slots when you have lectures. Then look at all the free time and decide how you will spend it.

Realise that your first year does count and then think how you will make it count in the best way possible.

Start taking things seriously. Realise *why* you are at university. Understand how much university can give you. Then start claiming what rightfully belongs to you.

Find work experience opportunities. Volunteer. Join societies and work for them – offer help without being asked, organise things, offer a helping hand whenever you can spare some time. Draw lessons from your activities. Think about what you have learnt. Extract valuable skills. Consider your studies and activities not as chores, but as chances to develop great skills for work and for life.

If you can't spare any time, you have to make some. Refuse evening TV. Forget computer games. And stop spending all those hours on Facebook – unless, of course, it is for professional purposes.

Make your Facebook profile professional. Build a comprehensive profile on LinkedIn. Join social networks for professional reasons.

Create a blog and write something that would be interesting and useful to others. Keep up the good work.

Say goodbye to your old life. Forget everything that you've learnt before because life starts anew here. And the best thing is – you are in charge of this life!

Get involved! Be seen!

Be awesome!

From Confusion to Conclusion

How to Write a First-Class Essay

Vlad Mackevic

This is a sample of another book of mine. It's called **From Confusion to Conclusion. How to Write a First-Class Essay.** *As you could guess by looking at the title and the cover, this one is on essay writing. I included extracts from it in this book as a 'trailer'. The book is available on Amazon.co.uk*

Why do you need to read this book?

Because you are at university. Because you are a student. Because you have to write an academic assignment. It's as simple as that.

Academic writing with its complex rules is hard to master fast. Essay titles can be confusing and you never know what your lecturers expect of you. You are constantly told to be more critical, but nobody bothers to explain what critical writing actually is. And all that tedious referencing! Why does every lecturer demand that you know everything?

In this book, Vlad Mackevic, a First Class graduate, shares his experience acquired whilst studying and working as an academic writing mentor.

This book will help you answer the following questions:

- How do you answer absolutely any essay (and exam) question?
- How do you create an easy-to-answer essay question for a free topic assignment or a dissertation?
- How do you write critically? And what does it even mean?
- Why do I need to write my introduction at the end?
- How do you make the research process as efficient as possible?
- How do you reference?

And many more. Enjoy reading and writing!

www.TheLectureRoom.co.uk
www.FirstYearCounts.com

From Confusion to Conclusion

How to Write a First-Class Essay

Vlad Mackevic

Edited by Tom Wild

Published in association with

www.FirstYearCounts.com

www.TheLectureRoom.co.uk

PREFACE

WHY ARE YOU reading this book?

Because you are at university. Because you are a student. Because you have to write an academic assignment. It's as simple as that. It doesn't even matter what kind of assignment it is. What matters is that you want to become better at what you're doing – and I want to thank you for choosing my book on your path to academic success. In this book, I promise to share all I know about essay, exam and dissertation writing.

In 2011, I graduated from Aston University, Birmingham, with a first-class degree in International Relations and English. During my four years at Aston, I worked in the university's Learning Development Centre, teaching my fellow students essay writing skills. During my placement year, I worked as a communications officer for The Science and Technology Facilities Council, spending my days writing promotional materials and my evenings writing a research project for university, as well as short stories (three of which were published in a small literary magazine). During my degree course, I also published three articles on linguistics in *Début: The Undergraduate Journal of Languages, Linguistics and Area Studies*.

In other words, *I've been there and done that*. I've got the scars, too! I have a lot of writing experience, both at university and outside of it. And here's what I can tell you.

The transition from school to university is not easy. All of a sudden, you're expected to obey all sorts of rules of writing that you had never heard of when you were at school. You have to write following a certain structure and using certain vocabulary; you're not allowed to say 'I think', and you have to

1

reference your work, which can make what you thought would be an expression of your creativity and ability to reason feel like simply repeating the findings of others.

It's not what you expect. It's tough. You have to learn to adapt. To make mistakes and learn through trial and error.

And the toughest part is not the research process or the referencing.

It's always the writing itself.

I'm writing this book because I want to help you become the best without going through what I went through. Without guessing and trying, without hitting and missing. After so many years, I know how university assignments work. Moreover, I know how to *make them work*.

I'm writing this book to make it easier for you to score 10-30% higher in *every* assignment you submit. Yes, I mean it! Because it's nothing but pure technique. The key is to become aware of what you're doing: how you're writing your assignments, what exactly you're doing well and whether there are any areas that need improvement. Once you start consciously applying the methods I outline in this book, you will boost your grades and be a first-class student before you know it.

My Story

Before I begin describing the techniques and giving you all sorts of useful tips, I want to give you some background information about my own academic and personal development.

When I started university, I initially enrolled on a Business Administration course. I completed a year, got a 70% average (mostly owing to the mathematics-based modules) and then decided it wasn't for me. I didn't like it, didn't feel passionate about it. If I had simply gritted my teeth and carried on, I could have succeeded as a business student, but it would have been a highly stressful three years.

I realised that I could only succeed doing something I felt passionate about – so I changed to International Relations and English. Yet, my love for the subjects was still not enough to get me a first.

In my first year, still on the business course, I faced an issue familiar to every student making the transition from sixth form or college to university: *I had no idea how to write academic assignments*.

I had the ability to memorise facts; I could learn by rote pretty well. Constant practice at school made me good at maths. Still, I knew nothing about the techniques that lead to academic success. Learning by heart was not enough for university.

When it was announced that we would have to submit a portfolio of two essays and ten other written tasks for one of our modules, all 400 first year undergraduate business students panicked. We were all inexperienced. We didn't have a clue about essay writing at university level! How could they expect us to produce dozens of pages of written work?

In order to write a first-class essay, you need more than a thorough knowledge of the subject or perfect grammar. There's something else that is much more important: *a set of tricks and techniques* that can make a good essay into a brilliant one – and which *no one* bothers to teach you at university! Usually, you find out these things when you get a mark that's lower than you expected. You go to your lecturer and they tell you where you went wrong. If you're lucky.

I learnt these tricks and techniques the hard way – and a strange way, too.

One of the best things that happened to me during my year studying business was unexpectedly getting a mark of 84% for my coursework. This helped me get the writing mentor's job in the university library. Yet, when I reflected upon it later, I realised that getting that mark was *sheer luck*. The luck of a novice.

Yes, I did get a high grade. Yes, I did write a good essay. But

I had no idea *how to do it again*.

I could correct basic, common-sense mistakes in an essay that needed improvement, but I didn't know how to consistently produce first-rate pieces of work. All I knew was that I had done something that worked and I could only hope that I might do it again.

Moreover, getting a writing mentor's job meant that I had to become an awesome employee – which also meant a great degree of responsibility. I no longer had the luxury of not knowing how first-class academic assignments are produced. So, I began studying my coursework portfolio, examining it from every angle, trying to pick out what I did well, bit by bit. I read books on essay writing and compared my own writing with what they advised.

It took me a long time to pick out all the features that led to my coursework success.

But I got there in the end.

At first, when I changed my degree course, my essay grades were hitting high and low sixties. It was close, but it was never a first. The luck of a novice was gone as well – I only scored over 80% once, in the final year, when I already knew all the tricks of the trade.

I got these marks because I knew the subject, not because I was good at assignment writing. But, as I realised more and more what I had done correctly, I started to apply the techniques I had identified in subsequent essays.

And then it started happening. Towards the second term of my first year studying International Relations and English, I started hitting seventies! Even for lazy, sloppy essays.

I finished university with a first class degree, three academic publications and a great work placement where I could apply my writing skills, under my belt.

In this book, I am going to tell you exactly what I did to succeed as a student without snapping from overwork!

I'll tell you something that you won't hear in lecture halls. I'll teach you the techniques that helped me land and keep the writing mentor's job and gave me the chance to pass on my knowledge and teach others what I knew. Once you figure them out, these techniques seem simple, but still, they are not that obvious. And for some reason, lecturers never tell you about them.

My academic and professional experience has equipped me with some basic knowledge that everyone should have. That's why I'm sharing it. I want to teach you how to succeed without trying too hard. It will still involve some work, but, if you know what to do and how to do it, it won't feel like hard labour!

Please note, however, that what I'm sharing is subjective. These techniques worked for me, but I cannot guarantee that you will get the same results, or that you will get 70% or more for each assignment if you only apply what I say in this book. A lot depends on your lecturer, specific aspects of your degree subject, the way you approach the assignment, and your own effort. However, I'm sure I can trust you on the last one – after all, if you are reading this book, it means you want to make an effort and succeed, and I am more than happy to help you.

As a writer, I know that writing is hard work. Academic assignments can sometimes feel a bit of a pain in the neck. I just want to make it easier for you. And, since I respect your time, I'll try to do this in about one hundred pages.

Basic knowledge. Pure technique. And some useful examples.

Let's get started!

CHAPTER 1

ACADEMIC WRITING: WHAT DO YOU GET MARKS FOR?

AT UNIVERSITY, YOU get marks for the following elements of your assignment:

- Answering the question
- Structure
- Style and language
- References
- Research and analysis
- Formatting and presentation

These elements are not listed in any order of importance. They are all equally important and every single one of them will earn you points – which all add up and amount to high grades. I will briefly explain each element.

1. Answering the Question

Despite the fact that this sounds obvious, everything you write in your assignment must be done with a sole purpose – answering the question. You have to make it relevant and informative. You must have evidence to back up your claims. The way you answer the question must be logical and coherent. Moreover, you must explain how each paragraph is related to the question or the topic of your assignment.

2. Structure

This is the 'formula', according to which you write your essay, research report or dissertation. It is a special way of organising your writing to make it flow coherently from the introduction to the conclusion. The majority of the chapters in this book deal with the building blocks of academic work – introduction, previous research, methodology, analysis, discussion and conclusion. In subsequent chapters, I will describe each of these, telling you what they consist of and how they should be written to make your academic writing more effective.

3. Style and Language

At university you are expected to write your assignments in 'proper English'. To do this you will need to know the difference between spoken and written language, how to write in appropriate academic style and avoid basic mistakes that make your essay look less professional. You will also need to learn to think and write like an academic.

This, however, does not mean you need to use big words and complicated sentences. Your writing can be plain and simple, and yet very impressive. See **Chapter 12: The Language of Academia** for more information.

4. References

The basic principle of referencing is as follows:

If you write about an idea that you did not come up with yourself, but which was taken from someone else's book or article, you have to give credit to that person and write their name next to the idea.

Referencing is all about respecting the work of others and not stealing someone else's thoughts. You can find more information on referencing in **Chapter 9: Referencing**.

5. Research and Analysis

This differs from subject to subject – so, there is a limit to how much I can help you with this. However, my own experience has taught me that the more you read on your subject, the deeper you will be able to think. *When you absorb other people's ideas, you generate ideas of your own.*

However, there is one vital aspect of deep analysis: *being critical.*

This means not believing the first source you read. Read different authors and examine their views on the subject. Are they similar or different? Moreover, how similar are their data and research methods to these you used? It also means acknowledging the limitations of your research. The theory you are using is not the only one; your data are never representative enough, and your method is not the only correct one either! For a more in-depth discussion, see **Chapter 7: Analysis and Discussion.**

6. Formatting and Presentation

If you invited your guests to dinner, you wouldn't serve them food on dirty plates.

The same applies to your essay. As your lecturer reads your work, sloppy formatting can be as insulting as a coffee stain across the page. Moreover, formatting usually constitutes five per cent of your mark, so a well-formatted and professionally presented essay can make a difference between a 2:1 and a first!

Make fonts uniform, leave wide margins, double-space your lines and add a conservative cover page – all of this is important. Read more about it in **Chapter 14: Formatting and Presentation.**

CHAPTER 2

THE STRUCTURE OF AN ACADEMIC ASSIGNMENT

THE FIRST THING you need to know about essays and dissertations is that they have a certain structure. There is a formula, a particular order in which academic works are written. Roughly speaking, the formula looks like this:

1. Introduction (10-15% of the word count)
2. Main Body (70-80% of the word count)
3. Conclusion (10-15% of the word count)

These three elements are rudimentary and will be analysed in depth in this book. However, before you begin any analysis, it is important to note **the two main principles on which academic assignments are built.** Depending on the assignment, this can be the **funnel principle** (this looks like a triangle with the tip pointing down) or the **hourglass principle** (two triangles with their tips touching). See the following pages for diagrams of these principles.

2.1. The Funnel and the Hourglass

The **funnel principle** (p. 12) implies a movement from broad to narrow. It is mostly used in academic essays with a set topic (see **Section 2.2.**). First, you describe the theory that is the focus of your essay in general strokes (usually it is the information you find in general textbooks and lecture slides), then you move on to the application of the theory, for example, referring to previous studies (you can find them in academic journals), and finally you examine these studies with a critical eye (your own view of the theory and its applications in relation to your assignment question).

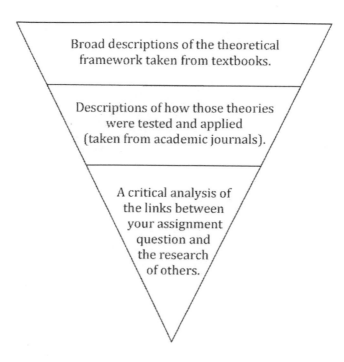

Figure 1: The funnel principle

The **hourglass principle** (p. 14) is very different. It usually applies to research assignments with a free topic, where you need to collect certain data and analyse it, such as research reports and dissertations. Your thoughts move from broad to narrow and back to broad again. Moreover, the numbered sections of the hourglass are interlinked.

Section 1 is linked to Section 6 – both discuss theory, but

the former gives a broad description of other researchers' theories while the latter focuses on how *your* research has enriched or reinforced the theoretical framework.

Section 2 is linked to Section 5 – both discuss the application of the theory, describing first how it was applied by others, and then discussing your own findings and how the two are related.

Finally, Section 3 is linked to Section 4, with you describing your data, methods and experiment design and then what you found post-experiment.

Both the funnel and the hourglass primarily reflect the structure of the main body of the assignment. The largest element of your essay, the main body, is made of a number of parts. There are some differences between academic essays with set topics and research papers/reports and dissertations, where you have to create your own research question. This is explained in the next two sections.

2.2. Analysing the Essay Question (Set Questions)

An academic essay is usually a written assignment with a **given (pre-set) topic.** You already know what the topic is – you just need to decipher it through breaking it down into its component parts and answer it.

An essay question is usually made of three parts: the **object** of the study, the **context** of the study and the **method** of the study. Let me explain this, using the following examples.

Example 1

Modern organisations often replace the traditional hierarchical structure with a more 'horizontal' team structure. Select two motivation theories from the field of organisational psychology and discuss how they can be applied in a team-based organisation.

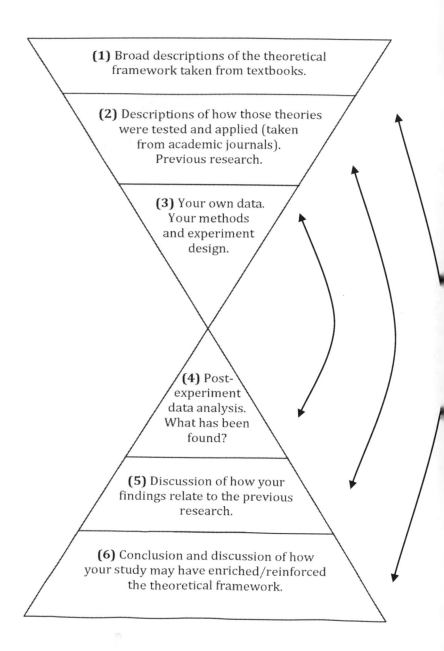

(1) Broad descriptions of the theoretical framework taken from textbooks.

(2) Descriptions of how those theories were tested and applied (taken from academic journals). Previous research.

(3) Your own data. Your methods and experiment design.

(4) Post-experiment data analysis. What has been found?

(5) Discussion of how your findings relate to the previous research.

(6) Conclusion and discussion of how your study may have enriched/reinforced the theoretical framework.

Figure 2: The hourglass principle

This essay question seems really complicated – primarily because the essay title is confusing. You don't know what the object, the context and the method of the study are. You need to *extract* them from the topic and separate them. Let's begin!

The object of the study

The object of your study is something with which you have to perform an *action*. Let's find the action by looking at the verbs in the question. We are only looking for the verbs in the imperative form – those that sound like orders, requests or commands. In this assignment, these words are *select* and *discuss*. Now, what do you need to select? *Two motivation theories.* This is your *object* of study. This is what you are going to analyse. But every kind of analysis needs to be performed in a specific context.

The context of the study

Context means *circumstances*. To find out the context, you need to ask the questions *When? Where? How?* and sometimes, *How much?*

In this essay question, you are not asked to discuss the general application of the two theories. Instead, you are asked to focus on a very specific context – team-based organisations that replace the traditional hierarchical structure with a horizontal team structure. In order to do this, you will naturally have to dedicate one or two paragraphs to describing the context. You will need to tell your reader what it means to have a team-based organisation. You will also need to define hierarchical structure. However, as this is only the context, do not spend too much time on describing it. Although it is very important and often intertwined with the object of the study, it is the background for your writing, but not the topic.

The method of the study

The method of your study is usually an *action*. It is expressed in verbs given in the imperative form. As already

15

mentioned these verbs are *select* and *discuss*. *Select* is pretty straightforward. However, *discuss* is more complex. It means look at the context in which the two theories were tested in the past (in hierarchically-structured organisations). Then look at the context of team-based organisations. Then look at the similarities and differences between these two contexts. And finally, based on this, write why these theories can and/or cannot be applied in modern organisations, taking into account all the differences between the traditional hierarchical structure and a team-based structure. Explain why it is possible or not possible each time.

When discussing, think of the following question: *Can the theories you are using be applied under **all** circumstances or not?* Or, more broadly, *Can **anything** be the case all the time?*

In other words, *discuss* means writing two opposing views and backing them up.

1. It *is* the case because

- Reason A
- Reason B
- Reason C

2. On the other hand, it is *not* the case because

- Reason A
- Reason B
- Reason C

You do not need to have the same number of reasons on both sides. In fact, you can have four reasons for and one against. The main objective is to demonstrate that you know that there are two opposing points of view (because there always are).

Please note that there is a separate section on 'method words' used in essay titles such as *discuss*, giving specific examples and explaining how to understand them in **Chapter 12: The Language of Academia**.

Example 2

What were the reasons for the economic miracle of South Korea in the second half of the twentieth century?

This essay question is pretty straightforward. However, it is worth keeping in mind that even questions like this involve something more than just listing the reasons you have found in the literature. Your lecturers normally expect you to either *present two opposing points of view* or *group your arguments according to certain criteria*.

So, let's start by finding the three elements:

The object of the study

Quite obviously, it is South Korea's economic development.

The context of the study

The context is the time-frame: the second half of the twentieth century. Therefore, you do not need to analyse what happened before this time (unless it led to vital changes in the second half of the twentieth century). Focus on events within the essay time-frame. Don't wander too far away from the essay question.

The method of the study

The method is not expressed as the imperative form of a verb this time. Rather, it is a noun – *reasons*. You need to *find the reasons* – but not just list them in any random order. In an ideal situation, your reasons should be grouped under two slightly opposing categories.

You can usually divide the reasons behind any change into two types: internal and external. It doesn't matter if the change happens at an individual level, the level of an organisation or at a national level.

I am not claiming that this rule is universal, but dividing arguments into two groups, the first involving internal processes in a social group, an organisation, or even a country, and the second related to the external context, is a good start for many assignments that ask you to list reasons.

Example 3

Name the advantages and disadvantages of administering drugs through the skin.

This assignment question is taken from the field of pharmacy/medicine, but a similarly structured question could be found in another area. For example, *What are the benefits and drawbacks of global computerisation?*

Questions like these have no 'yes' or 'no' answer. They have even fewer parts than the previous ones. The **context** of the study is usually implied – it is *now*. You are asked to discuss current events and all your research should be actual rather than historical. Both drug delivery through the skin and global computerisation are happening *now*.

The **object** of the study is also clear – it is drug delivery through the skin in the first question and global computerisation in the second one.

The **method** of the study is finding and naming the advantages and disadvantages. The number of benefits and drawbacks doesn't have to be equal. However, you have to acknowledge that both benefits and drawbacks do exist.

2.3. The Structure of Research Reports and Dissertations

Research reports and dissertations are structured differently from essays. First of all, they do not have a given topic. Normally, you are expected to come up with your own research question. This changes the entire approach to writing because it adds certain elements that are absent from an essay with a set question – but I will deal with this issue in due course.

Listed below are the elements that comprise a research report or a dissertation and where they are covered in this book:

- **Topic or title** – how to create a simple, manageable topic for your research (**Chapter 3**)

- **Introduction** – how to write one and why it's best to write it when you have completed the essay (**Chapter 4**)

- **Literature Review** (also known as 'Previous Research') – why you need one and how to write it (**Chapter 5**)

- **Methodology** – how to collect your data, what research methods you can use and how to use participants in your study (**Chapter 6**)

- **Research** – how you conduct it, what you need to be aware of, quantitative and qualitative research and which research methods are most appropriate (**Chapter 6**)

- **Analysis and Discussion** – what analysis and discussion mean, how you can be critical about your data, why you need to find weaknesses in your research and how you write about them (**Chapter 7**)

- **Conclusion** – how to write a strong ending and leave a long-lasting impression on your readers (**Chapter 8**)

- **References** – why you need to reference and how to do it, with some useful websites with free resources (**Chapter 9**)

These are the basic elements. However, you also need to take into account certain aspects that are common to all academic assignments.

Chapter 10: What About Exams? deals with exam writing strategies. In many disciplines there are so-called 'essay style' exams, where students literally have to write a coherent essay in response to an exam question within a limited amount of time. **Chapter 10** provides tips for successfully passing these exams.

Chapter 11: The Writing Process explains how to make the writing process smoother, covering techniques such as note-taking, active reading, outlining and brainstorming. It teaches you how to write more efficiently.

Chapter 12: The Language of Academia explains how to understand action words in academic assignments and what the language and style of your essay should be like.

Chapter 13: Writing Tips is a broad discussion of advice on writing. It is made up of three parts:

(1) The Researcher's Point of View gives advice on how to conduct better research, provides resources for research and gives general academic advice.

(2) The Grammarian's Point of View focuses on correct spelling and grammar and lists basic mistakes that you should avoid in your writing.

(3) The Writer's Point of View explains the process of academic writing from a writer's perspective. Writing an academic essay is hard so the tips in this section will make life easier for you.

Chapter 14: Formatting and Presentation deals with the basic visual elements of an academic assignment. Do you want to know how to present your work in a professional manner? Read this chapter and find out.

So, this is how the book is going to be structured from this point on. And now – let's get down to business.

ABOUT THE AUTHOR

VLAD MACKEVIC is an author entrepreneur, an academic writing expert and an employability consultant. He writes fiction for the soul (under the pen-name Roy Eynhallow) and non-fiction for the mind. In 2011, he graduated from Aston University, Birmingham with a First Class degree in International Relations and English Language. This book was written to sum up Vlad's professional experience and to share it with you for your benefit and enjoyment.

Connect to Vlad online:

Websites
www.FirstYearCounts.com
www.TheLectureRoom.co.uk

For Fiction (pen name Roy Eynhallow)
www.EynhallowBooks.com

Facebook
https://www.facebook.com/First.year.counts

Twitter
http://twitter.com/Vlad_Mackevic
http://twitter.com/EynhalowBooks

LinkedIn
http://www.linkedin.com/in/vladmackevic

15983341R00071

Made in the USA
Charleston, SC
29 November 2012